Dear Drew.
Continue to live in
The Joy A.A.C.T.!

Love
Lisa Summerour

DIVORCE
IS NOT A
DESTINATION®

A.A.C.T. In Joy!™

Advance Praise

Dr. Summerour writes beautifully and grippingly. I feel her compassion, empathy, and wisdom permeate my mind as I read this book. She utilizes narrative storytelling, cognitive pedagogy, and through these, imparts clarity, calm, and peace. She makes healing seem doable and indeed, she herself has demonstrated that it is.

APRIL POWELL-WILLINGTON, Mother, Deputy Attorney General, Partnership for Peace & Transformative Impact – Board of Directors Chair

More than a guide, *Divorce Is Not A Destination* is a lifeline for anyone going through or working to get over a divorce or breakup. The empowering reflections encourage much needed self-awareness and personal accountability. Dr. Lisa challenges you to dispel beliefs about divorce that no longer serve you. One of the many strengths of *Divorce Is Not A Destination* lies in the practical tips and tools that teach you to decrease anxiety, whether it's from anticipating difficult conversations with an ex or talking to a child about life events that also impact them. Reading about the challenges faced by teenage mothers through the decades and unconventional perspectives on biblical references to divorce resonated with me deeply.

GWENDOLYN OGLESBY-ODOM, Ed.D., MSN, RN-BC, NEA-BC, Mother of Two, Healthcare Executive, Board Director

As I turned the pages of *Divorce Is Not A Destination*, I found myself nodding in recognition, each word a testament to the transformative journey I had experienced after my own divorce. Dr. Lisa's "A.A.C.T. in Joy!" framework - Accountability, Alignment, Communicate and Trust - mirrored the life-changing lessons I learned. Embracing Accountability inspired me to take ownership of my life. Aligning my values with my actions gave me courage to truly live as God called me to live. Learning and practicing how to Communicate clearly, both with my internal voice and with others, helped me to better understand 'me' and build healthier relationships. Learning to Trust myself again and the wisdom God gave me instilled unshakable confidence in me that I apply to all aspects of my life.

Dr. Lisa validated my decision to prioritize my wellbeing and affirmed that leaving an unhealthy marriage was necessary for rediscovering who I truly am. Other women's stories and experiences made me feel part of a supportive community, combating the isolation divorce often brings.

I encourage readers to do the exercises, especially writing your own story with yourself as the heroine. This process will help you reclaim your story and embrace your inner resilience. If you're grappling with the complexities of divorce, *Divorce Is Not A Destination* offers a compassionate roadmap for navigating the journey with grace, A.A.C.T. in Joy! You'll find solace, inspiration, and the strength to create a life of peace and joy on the other side…as I and so many others have.

TISH BALDEZ, Mother of Three Grown Men and Managing Partner, P31 Consulting, LLC

What I love, first, and foremost, about Dr. Lisa's approach to navigating divorce is how she teaches you to alchemize the experience from a death into a rebirth. She does this with such refreshing humor, honesty, and tenderness, so that by the time you are done reading, you feel like Dr. Lisa understands that the grieving heart needs a certain amount of busy work, and even focal points, to help move through it. She expertly coaches you through practical and insightful exercises and writing prompts so you can return to a deeper and richer sense of your own authenticity. She not only teaches you how to survive, but also how to thrive and dream again.

I also love how Dr. Lisa illustrates how family and ancestral patterns contribute to the complicated dynamics of our relationships through her own captivating storytelling. In weaving her full self into the fabric of *Divorce Is Not A Destination,* we find a trustworthy guide to help us navigate through the night sea journey of divorce to find joy once again.

> *DR. SHANNON SLOAN-SPICE, Mother, Eco-therapist, Educator, Artist, and Somalchemist*

Dr. Lisa Summerour has a unique ability to connect directly to the heart of a situation. The personal stories of her experiences in life with partners, family, friends, and colleagues warm the heart and inspire the soul. (My divorce occurred after 38 years of marriage.) In reading *Divorce is Not A Destination*, I felt as if she was speaking to me. While addressing my many fears and exposing many of the misconceptions related to being Divorced, she empowered me. This empowerment will enable me to reflect, appreciate, and, most of all, improve myself going forward.

> *VAL CHANCELLOR, Sports and Entertainment Marketing (retired)*

"Wow! *Divorce Is Not A Destination* really struck a chord with me on so many levels. The thought-provoking questions prompted some deep introspection. The personal stories were like heartfelt conversations with a friend over coffee. I loved how the combination of self-help and biography kept me eager to get to the next chapter. And the geek in me appreciated the fascinating facts and tidbits.

I've been married for 27 years, and *Divorce Is Not A Destination* still resonated with me. Dr. Lisa helped me re-evaluate divorcing a career after two decades and a friendship that went back 35 years. Being accountable to my well-being has never been clearer than it is after reading *Divorce Is Not A Destination*. Dr. Lisa opened my eyes to perspectives I had not considered, and the process has given me much-needed clarity. I feel better equipped to move beyond these experiences to expecting and embracing inner joy!

A. CASEY, Sporting Facility Franchise Owner,
Wife and Mother of Two

Reading *Divorce Is Not A Destination* was an eye-opening experience for me as a single woman. It helped me realize the importance of addressing relationship issues early on and not waiting until it's too late. This book challenged my preconceptions about divorce within my family and encouraged me to take accountability for my actions, even in the aftermath of a breakup. It reminded me that divorce isn't just the end of a relationship; it's an opportunity for growth and redefining how we continue forward, whether through healthy co-parenting or setting boundaries. *Divorce Is Not A Destination* also provided valuable insights into preparing for the unexpected, equipping me with the knowledge and tools needed to navigate both the emotional and practical aspects of divorce should I ever find myself in that situation. It's like having an emergency kit for life's uncertainties, ensuring I'm not left feeling lost but empowered to face whatever challenges come my way.

S ZAHIR, Registered Nurse

I worked with Dr Lisa for several months after a very difficult marriage break up. She helped me immensely, enabling me to find my way through my divorce and on to my new chapter. I've become more confident and have more trust in my decision making. She has helped me communicate well with my teenage son through this process. She has enabled me to spot helpful and unhelpful patterns in my behaviour and to change unhelpful thoughts into more productive ones. I used the tools I learned to change how I responded to and communicated with my ex during and after our divorce, which alleviated a lot of stress for me. I'm proud of the behavior I model for my son, and I'm proud of taking accountability for my life. Dr. Lisa helped me to see and appreciate the person I am today. When I started working with Dr. Lisa, returning to work seemed impossible. Today, I'm happy to say I've made a successful return to a job that I love.

JENNY R., Coaching Client (United Kingdom)

DIVORCE
IS NOT A
DESTINATION®

A.A.C.T. In Joy!™

A Path to Overcoming Heartache,
Rebuilding Confidence,
and Living with Joy – After Breakup

Dr. Lisa Summerour
BREAKUP & DIVORCE COACH

Divorce Is Not A Destination®
© 2024 Lisa D. Summerour

Some names have been changed to protect people's privacy.

Published 2024

Logo Design by DK Graphics
Cover Design by Mykola Shelepa
Cover Photos by MiaMeesha -The Perfect Shot
Book Layout Design by Penny Dawson

Printed in the United States

Library of Congress Cataloging-in-Publication Data

Names: Summerour, Lisa D. Author
Title: Divorce Is Not A Destination: A.A.C.T. In Joy! – a path to overcoming heartache, rebuilding confidence, and living with joy – after breakup /Lisa D. Summerour.
Description: Fallbrook, CA

Identifiers: Library of Congress Catalog Number (LCCN) 2024907749 Hardcover ISBN 9781961233003 | eBook ISBN 9781961233010 | Paperback ISBN 9781961233027

Subjects: Self-help Personal Growth - Self-Esteem | Self-help Personal Growth - Happiness | Self-help Personal Growth – General

To my nieces: Tahira, Fatimah, Kareemah, Frances, Alise, Latifa, Nikki, Kim, LaTasha, Lakeesha, Chanelle, and Renee,

May you embrace the lessons within these pages about family, resilience, and growth. Learn from our experiences, including our mistakes, so that you may navigate life's challenges with wisdom and strength. My prayer is for you to remember that love, self-discovery, and inner strength are the keys to building a life filled with joy and fulfillment.

Love Auntie

Contents

Glossary i

Introduction v

1 Divorced at Four 1

2 Permission to Grieve 5

3 When Grown Folk Talk 23

4 A.A.C.T. In Joy! 37

5 Children and Change 69

6 Seven Things to Help You Right Now 81

7 Rites of Passage 95

8 A Personal – Personnel Problem 107

9 Create a Vision Network 117

10 In A.A.C.T.ion 127

11 Divorced and Dynamic 141

12 Journey to Joy 157

Bibliography 165

Connect 167

Offering 167

Acknowledgements 169

About the Author 171

After my divorce, I was struggling to find my own voice. Through reading, I gained my power back."

— HALLE BERRY

Glossary

Accountability: The state of being answerable or responsible for one's actions, decisions, or performance, often involving the obligation to explain or justify these actions to others. DINAD: Accepting responsibility for your life today is key to empowering yourself.

Alignment: The state of agreement, harmony, or synchronization between individuals, groups, or entities in terms of goals, objectives, values, or strategies.

Aspirations: Strong desires, ambitions, or long-term visions that motivate and drive individuals towards achieving specific goals or fulfilling certain dreams.

Authenticity: The quality of being genuine, sincere, and true to oneself or to one's values and beliefs, characterized by honesty and transparency in actions and interactions; Being who you really are, not pretending to be someone else because of what other people think.

Communication: The process of exchanging information, thoughts, ideas, or feelings between individuals or groups through verbal or non-verbal means, such as speaking, writing, facial expressions, body movement and hand gestures.

Divorce: The legal dissolution or termination of a marriage or marital relationship, resulting in the separation of spouses and the dissolution of marital duties and responsibilities; To separate or dissociate from something, someplace or someone.

Goals: Desired outcomes or achievements that individuals or organizations strive to attain. This is the proverbial pot of gold at the end of the rainbow; the idea of moving on or breaking away from something once closely connected.

Happiness: is generally associated with a feeling of contentment, satisfaction, or pleasure derived and linked to specific external events, achievements, or situations that bring about positive emotions; typically, transient and can fluctuate based on changing circumstances or external factors. It tends to be more surface-level and may involve a range of positive emotions like excitement, pleasure, or comfort.

Joy: Deeper and more profound than happiness independent of external circumstances. often characterized by a sense of inner peace, fulfillment, or spiritual well-being; it can be sustained even during challenging times or in the absence of specific positive experiences. It is rooted in gratitude, contentment, and a deeper connection to oneself or others.

Objectives: Specific, measurable steps or targets that support achieving your goals. If you think S.M.A.R.T. Goals should be called S.M.A.R.T. Objectives, I agree.

Self: The essential, individual identity and consciousness of a person; the distinct personality, thoughts, emotions, and experiences that define one's unique existence.

Surviving self (lowercase s): quick to judge and take things personally and always ready for a fight – attacking, provoking, protecting, or blaming itself or others. It believes the image in the mirror is all there is, so it fears for its life. (Tina Lifford)

Thriving Self (uppercase S): Sees situations as opportunities to grow and expand; believes anything is possible and everything can change for the better. It dwells in energies such as hope, possibility, enthusiasm, and gratitude. (Tina Lifford)

Trust: The belief, confidence, or reliance placed in yourself, someone, or something based on integrity, reliability, honesty, and consistency of behavior or performance. Trust implies a willingness to be vulnerable or depend on others.

Vision Board: A creative expression and physical manifestation that supports your intentional actions toward desired objectives. Use the board to connect your thinking and senses to outcomes so you strengthen your motivation to achieve them.

Vulnerability: Your willingness to show up and be seen even when there are no guarantees. Part of it is about being susceptible to emotional harm or verbal criticism. Another part is about embracing courage and openness in the face of uncertainty, risk, and emotional exposure.

Introduction

Thunderous lightning strikes a giant oak.

The massive tree falls in slow motion toward the street. Onlookers stare in shock.

The crashing sound echoes above screeching brakes.

Everything vibrates as the tree falls to the pavement, grazing cars, terrorizing drivers, and blocking rush hour traffic in both directions.

This is what divorce feels like. A damaging, devastating derailment of your life, replete with onlookers gawking at the wreckage.

There is an added sense of exposure and sensitivity when you have experienced divorce more than once like me. Initially, my four marriages wear like a patchwork coat of embarrassment. Obvious proof of my failings and personal dysfunction. There was a time when living with the stigma of several divorces resulted in self-imposed misery. A misery borne from basking in the darkness of other people's judgement.

Like many situations and events viewed through the lens of society, people's perceptions and beliefs shape my feelings about divorce. Church members and some family members feel compelled to share with me that divorcing is bad. And it happens to irresponsible people who make rash decisions and give up too easily. People who don't respect the institution of marriage. What I conclude is: being divorced more than once means something must be wrong with me. Right? Right.

It would take decades to identify the stops and starts my divorces create in my life. Stops and starts that disintegrate my confidence and leave me questioning my ability to make sound decisions.

As proof of the multifaceted aspect of life, while my personal life may have been described as "being in a shambles", other aspects of my life soar.

Nana always encouraged me to try anything. She would say,

"Do it. Whatever it is, do it. You don't want to be 74 years old and look back over your life saying, 'I wonder what would've happened if ...'"

It is Nana's encouragement and this mindset that move me to enter the Miss New Jersey USA Pageant. An unexpected experience that leads to me becoming the first Black woman crowned Miss New Jersey USA in 1986. This is also how I meet pageant director and force of nature, Marilyn Sietz. Our relationship opens me to a world of opportunities and a lifelong friendship. One of the opportunities I'm introduced to through Marilyn is acting.

My final decision to take a leap of faith into a career I had only remotely dreamt of came after receiving advice and encouragement from my godfather, Larry James Avery, the beloved father on *The Fresh Prince of Bel Air*. A classically trained actor, jazz enthusiast, and lifelong family friend, who admittedly rarely gave actors advice, advised me to:

"Learn your lines, be on time, and always respect the crew. Find a way to do theatre because it's hard work that doesn't pay well. If you still want to be an actor after that, you just might make it. You're an actor. It doesn't matter if it's Shakespeare, film, television, or standing on a soap box on 42nd street. Your job is to act."

It is through Marilyn and working with her pageant organization that I meet agents, casting directors, and eventually, Richard Scanlon. An actor and acting instructor based in New York; it is Richard who prepares me for an audition that lands me in a program at the acclaimed Freedom Theatre in Philadelphia. Uncle Larry is right—life theatre is a lot of work. I love it. The experience hones my acting skills and boosts my confidence.

Eventually, I secure agency representation with two well-respected agencies in the industry, J. Michael Bloom and APA in New York. I land my first role playing opposite Denzel Washington in the Academy Award nominated film *Philadelphia*. I go on to land roles opposite Forrest Whitaker in *The Enemy Within*, Chi McBride and Bruce Willis in *Mercury Rising*, and Bruce Willis again in *The Sixth Sense*.

My moderate success in direct sales lands me in leadership. Exposure, my writing, and speaking ability catch the attention of the executives. This leads me to hosting a regional event and paves the way for my national speaking debut. My exit from the Minneapolis Convention Center Stage is accompanied by the applause of nearly 4000 sales representatives. Down the side steps and behind the stage, I'm greeted by the keynote speaker who is up next.

He listens to my entire presentation from backstage. He greets me with,

"This is exactly what you should be doing."

These days, my skepticism would usually kick in, and I'd figure out some way to dismiss or deflect this compliment. Not this time. He is soberly sincere. He is also David McNally, the author of *Even Eagles Need a Push*, and National Hall of Fame Speaker. There's no reason for him to lie and every reason for me to believe him.

I felt like I belonged on that stage, sharing with that audience.

I have coached C-suite executives, advised CEOs, written a curriculum for leaders at an international event in Ghana, and traveled to Uganda as the Strategic Advisor to the CEO of an international consulting firm. Some would say my work experience is all over the place. Others might say it speaks to the diverse nature of my gifts. I'm good with eclectic.

All this is important because it's easy for people to assume that multiple divorces would equate to a completely dysfunctional life. In fact, I have accomplished quite a lot. It's almost like living two different lives.

There's the one life that people admire, and some admit to envying. Then there's the other side where I feel people wonder, *what is wrong with her? Why can't she get it together?* If this sounds like you, you're reading the right book.

In these pages, I will share personal stories and revelations. I hope that my vulnerability will encourage you to be vulnerable with yourself. This is a process. And I begin the process with family.

When I examine my family history, I realize divorce seems to be woven into my family's DNA. Does that make my family more dysfunctional than any other? I don't know. I do know that by examining my family's story, I found a pathway to appreciating my life.

Writing *Divorce Is Not A Destination* is my way of reaching out to people who feel guilt or shame because they've divorced or are on the brink of divorce. This is also for the person who has had breakups that have impacted them so negatively, they struggle with rebuilding self-confidence. Ending an unfulfilling, and sometimes damaging, relationship is being responsible. It's being true to ourselves and to our own needs. We don't relinquish our right to joy because we end a marriage.

As a master practitioner and accredited breakup and divorce coach, I am committed to educating people. Neither you nor I set out to dismantle the institution of marriage. No more so than me dropping out of college was an attempt at dismantling higher education. Some things work and some things do not.

Today, I can explain what I didn't understand as a teen or well into my thirties. Joy is my birthright. And when I make joy the journey, I end up there every time. Pain, suffering, and disappointment are inescapable aspects of life.

What I want for you is what I've achieved for myself. A confidence that comes from knowing who I am, whose I am, and a belief that the possibilities in my life are endless. I cannot be defined by the things that surround me, and I won't be defined by mindsets that bound me to other peoples' expectations or limitations. What I know to be true, is that with the right support and tools, you can overcome heartache, rebuild your confidence, and live a life of joy after a breakup.

Writing *Divorce Is Not A Destination* is a look beyond more than forty years of intimate relationships to explore family dynamics to understand what I learned about marriage and divorce before I ever said, "I do."

In *Divorce Is Not A Destination*, I identify four foundational elements that helped me shed the weight of other people's expectations, honor my emotions, and find ways to empower myself. Experiment with what you learn in this book, and you will find your footing along the path of your journey to joy.

The first element is embracing **Accountability.** Accepting responsibility for your life today is key to empowering yourself. Empowerment is about permitting yourself to change and believing that you are the agent of change in your life.

Next, is creating **Alignment** between your values and how you're showing up in the world. This is where you ask yourself the question: Am I honoring what I say matters to me?

The third area is learning to **Communicate** clearly and guilt-free. This includes your inner dialogue as well as how you communicate with others.

Finally, learning to **Trust** Self. Your ability to trust yourself impacts your confidence and influences your ability to trust others.

In *Divorce Is Not A Destination* I share experiences, stories, and lessons I've learned. I invite you to experiment with ideas, tools, and resources that have helped me, and others navigate to joy beyond our breakups and divorces.

My desire is that you:

- Are encouraged to explore new ways of thinking about your breakup or divorce experience.

- Review your family history of marriage and divorce.

- See your breakup or divorce as part of your life's journey, not a dead end.

- Be empowered by your story, not imprisoned by it.

- Understand that you control what you think and how you feel about what you think.

- Examine, redefine, and realign your thinking with your values.

- Realize that the world can't steal your joy if you're living it.

Today, I embrace my niece calling me a Renaissance woman. No more hiding my light because I'm afraid of what people will discover about me. I cannot and will not be shamed by my life. My divorces helped shape me, but they alone do not define me.

Live in the joy of your life. When you do, you will learn that divorce does not mean you are damaged, defective, defeated, or done living. Your journey continues because divorce is not a destination.

CHAPTER 1

Divorced at Four

Divorce is a journey that the children involved do not ask to take. They are forced along for a ride where the results are dictated by the road their parents decide to travel.

— DIANE GREENE

When you pack in a rush, you don't have time for boxes. At four years old, I'm riding in the back section of a station wagon surrounded by piles of unboxed books. I love being surrounded by these books.

The car turns off the road. My back is to the window facing the property. Turning my head and shoulders as far as I can, I catch a glimpse of the largest house I've ever seen.

We're not moving. We've moved.

Me, my sister, and mommy have left the apartment we lived in with daddy. I don't know how far we've driven; I just know it's too far. Too far for mommy to walk us to Mama Ida's house before she heads off to high school. Too far for Granddaddy to take me for drives passing neighbors who smile and wave at us cruising by in his always shiny Chevy. And too far for me to eat Mama Ida's fried apples. The ones she'd send us to pick from the tree at the end of the fence, growing on the edge of the driveway opposite Grandaddy's well-manicured lawn.

Our move divorces us from the quaint all Black community of Lincoln Park. When it was founded in 1891, it was the only area in Montgomery County, Maryland, where Blacks could purchase land. Every lot in Lincoln Park is owned by somebody who looks like me and my family. Cognitively, I don't understand the implications of any of this at four years of age. Being submerged in the richness of Black pride, love, family, community, and respect shape my perspective long before I know what perspective is. The radiant reality of my childhood remains a source of fond memories. The pride in knowing that my family comes from a place where Black people own their homes, cars, and businesses means everything. They run the churches where they worship, teach in the schools their children attend, and maintain the cemetery where loved ones are laid to rest.

None of this shields me from experiencing the impact of divorce long before I ever know what divorce is, and years before my parents formally file for one.

The Far Away Place

My grandparents are Margaret Elizabeth (Pinkett) and Henry Magruder. As the oldest grandchild, I name them by default. Because of me, she will forever be known as Nana. And because I can't make the "r" sound when I start talking, my grandfather is hereto dubbed Gampy instead of Grampy.

Nana and Gampy's home is a two-story house sitting on an acre of land that they purchased from Mr. Love. I have no idea how old Mr. Love is. I know he is white. And I'm sure he's the oldest person I've ever seen. Which makes it official, Mr. Love is an old white man.

The story of how Nana and Gampy purchase a lot of Mr. Love's land for $1 is family history and my first lesson on race relations. I hear about how some white people didn't want a Black family moving into their neck of the woods. The first lot my grandparents purchase when they decide to move from Rockville, Maryland to New Jersey, qualifies because it is literally in the woods.

Through the years, family members take turns driving me to the lot while retelling the story of how white people burned the house to the ground when it was under construction. Always sad as they point to the charred remains of the foundation, remembering what might've been. Mimicking their solemn posture seems appropriate. Oh, but inside, I feel relieved that the big house ended up on Fire Road, not on this scary dirt road in the middle of nowhere surrounded by all these trees.

The one dollar transaction happens after Mr. Love and Nana meet at the municipal building. Mr. Love overhears Nana relay to the clerk that their home had been destroyed while under construction. Long story short, that old white man decides to sell a young Black couple an acre of land for $1.

I am too young to know the word racism. I do understand meanness and anger. I don't understand why anyone would be mean or angry at Nana and Gampy's house. Fortunately, I also know it isn't all white people because Mr. Love is an old white man, and his kindness makes it possible for my grandparents to build a home that would anchor our family for generations. For now, the big house on Fire Road is the destination at the end of my first divorce-inspired journey.

What changed in your life because of divorce?

Take a few minutes and write down one significant change that happened in your life because of a divorce. It could be your divorce, your parents', or your grandparents'. Avoid judging the change or its impact. For now, just identify the situation and how it impacted you.

How do you remember feeling about the change when it happened?

How do you feel about it today?

CHAPTER 2

Permission to Grieve

"There is no pain or failure like going through a divorce."

— JENNIFER LOPEZ

Jackie's Grief

The only thing open wider than the eyes staring back at me is the door I open to let the hospice worker in for their shift.

"Hello," I say warmly.

James hesitates before crossing the threshold. His eyes narrow as they search mine for an answer to a question he's trying desperately not to ask. I smile.

His eyes dart through the dining room to the railing above my parents' sunken living room. Just below the railing is the hospital bed my dad has lived in for the past several weeks. James, no matter how hard he peers, can't see over the railing to know if the bed is empty or not.

Perry hasn't eaten in nearly ten days and hasn't had water in about seven. Hospice care workers have repeatedly braced us for his death over the past week.

Before crossing the threshold, James asks, "Is he …?"

He pauses long enough that I finish the sentence, "… still alive?"

He stares, uncomfortable and unsure if he should be embarrassed or guilt-ridden for being so obvious.

Continuing, I answer, "Yes, he is."

I smile and laugh softly. I smile to ease James' discomfort. I chuckle at the realization that the Marine lying in that bed will not allow death or medical norms to tell him when to die.

My parents have been married for forty-two years. Between them are two ex-wives, one ex-husband, seven children, three relocations to three states, four home purchases, a half dozen or more jobs, at least one affair, and two miscarriages. The years haven't all been easy.

My mother once told me, "Our marriage isn't perfect, but we've done more for our children together than either of us would have accomplished alone." Theirs is a marriage of love and practicality woven together so beautifully that the lines are forever blurred as to which came first, or which matters most. Love or practicality.

The day comes. It's early morning. Soon, there will be a shift change, and our favorite hospice care worker, Marie, will arrive. For now, we prepare. There's just enough room for my mother to fit between the wall and the hospital bed. No more attempts to get him to sip water or suck ice. No more late nights playing gospel jazz, anticipating him slipping into eternity listening to Kirk Whalum and Jonathan Butler only to awake and find him alive and less well. This time, we know. I'm on the opposite side of the bed as I watch my mom take his hand in hers as he takes his last breath. It is October 23, 2014.

The Big "D"

There is something about experiencing the death of a loved one that fosters in us the capacity for empathy, sympathy, forgiveness, concern, and a host of other emotions to flow. We anticipate these emotions from others, and we offer them to ourselves graciously when we lose someone we care about.

We grant ourselves and others permission to experience the natural range of emotions brought on by grief. We are graciously supportive and concerned when grief leads to sleep deprivation, not eating enough or overeating, sadness, difficulty concentrating, or depression. There are no boundaries to the idiosyncrasies we make room for when we suffer the loss of a loved one through death.

The Other "D"

The loss of a loved one through divorce is different. Other than instances of abuse or overtly toxic relationships, and even sometimes despite them, we don't view the loss resulting from divorce in the same way we do with death. Not for others, and not for ourselves.

Olga's Loss

"I don't need coaching. I didn't want to do this because I don't want to dredge up stuff I've already dealt with."

That is how the coaching session with Olga begins.

A successful physician with a private practice, Olga lives in a beautiful resort-like community. She is an example of what it's like when we try to convince ourselves that we're fine when we're everything but fine.

Approximately 90 minutes into our session, Olga's eyes fill with tears. Holding her gaze, I give her a minute before asking,

"What just happened?"

Olga reveals emotions around her divorce, the death of a dear friend, and several other traumatic events she's experienced. She shares feelings and thoughts she has submerged for more than a decade.

Submerging emotions is a coping mechanism. In the long term, it is neither effective nor healthy. Researchers and wellness practitioners agree that unresolved emotional suffering can manifest into health issues, including immune system deficiencies, depression, PTSD, hypertension, and more.

Jackie and Olga are dealing with the top two items on the Holmes-Rahe Life Stress Inventory list. The death of a spouse is listed as the most stressful life event a person can experience. The second most stressful life event is divorce.

Emotions left to fester often manifest in other ways. During our session, I invite Olga to give herself permission to grieve the loss she experienced because of death as well as the loss she experienced through her divorce.

Like Olga, many individuals have an easier time dispensing grace when it comes to the death of a loved one. Not so much when they are processing loss due to a breakup or divorce.

People who continue to perpetuate family dynamics where expressing certain emotions is frowned upon may struggle. The child taught not to cry when they are clearly in emotional or physical pain, grew up in that family. The successful person taught that being assertive and speaking up for themselves is mannish, unattractive, and aggressive, they too grew up in that family. Countless numbers of people grew up getting reprimanded for bragging or being prideful, when they were merely acknowledging their own gifts and talents.

One of the things I hope you take away from reading *Divorce Is Not A Destination* is the importance of you loving and appreciating yourself. If this is foreign to you, I ask that you give yourself permission to experience loving yourself. Acknowledging the unique attributes you bring to the world, is a good place to start. Think of three things you appreciate about yourself.

Write them here:

1.

2.

3.

You can also download my free guide From Divorced to Dynamically (Positive. Energetic. Innovative.) You!®. This guide will walk you through three exercises designed to reveal positive attributes you should be proud of. Visit www.divorceisnotadestionation.com and go to Resources.

Now that you know losing a spouse and going through a divorce rank #'s 1 and 2 on the Holmes-Rahe Life Stress Inventory, my hope is you show yourself some grace as you go through the stages of the loss cycle related to your breakup or divorce.

Grief and Loss

Psychiatrist Elisabeth Kubler-Ross identified five stages of grieving in her 1969 book *On Death and Dying*. The stages were denial, anger, bargaining, depression, and acceptance. She later revised the list to include shock and testing.

Personally, understanding the different stages has been immensely helpful to me. Identifying, discussing, and giving myself permission to experience these stages, empowered me and eliminated the feelings of helplessness. This is my wish for you as you gain insights from this chapter.

Your Way Is the Right Way

The grieving process is not linear. In other words, you may not experience them in a specific order. It's also possible that you will not experience all seven stages, and you may cycle through one or more stages, more than once. It's beneficial to view the stages as descriptive rather than prescriptive. Look at the stages as ways to describe your emotional state as you process the loss or losses you experience because of your divorce.

Finally, know that you cannot fail at grieving. Avoid putting pressure on yourself to *get it right*. My hope is that you become aware of your emotions and learn to sit with them so you can understand what they can teach you. Know that you are not alone. The emotions you're experiencing are a normal part of the Loss Cycle, and hopefully, you find comfort in having a language to describe what you're feeling.

<u>Shock</u>

Shock may describe that initial response you have when you realize divorce is imminent. You might feel numb or frozen. The blood drains from your face, and you feel light-headed. Your heartbeat races as your anxiety level rises. Your chest tightens. For some, it's an adrenaline rush. For others, it's the biggest energy drain ever.

Shock is what I feel when I realize my first husband, *the voice,* has infected me with herpes. We are engaged and planning our wedding. Being in that euphoric engagement stage, my first thought is how much I appreciate him for telling me. *Isn't this a sign of trust?* Unroll your eyes and stop judging me.

The second thought that enters my mind is, *why has it taken him so long into our relationship to tell me?* It takes a few days for me to come to the disappointing and devastating realization that he told me because he thought he infected me. And he has.

I've always been sensitive to my body changing, so I know something is wrong. At that moment, I vacillate between focusing on the sense of betrayal I feel, the discomfort from my first outbreak, and the shame I

Divorce Is Not A Destination®

am already experiencing at having a disease everyone views as, cue scary music: *the worst sexually transmitted disease you could get because it's incurable!*

My shock is the "I can't believe this is happening to me" and "I can't believe he did this to me" kind of shock. I am also scared. After the initial wave of panic passes over me, I set out to learn everything I can about herpes. One of the members of the support group I locate has been married for years. She's had children and said she's never infected her husband. Her two children were born without being infected during childbirth. Hearing her story gives me confidence that I will live without feeling eternally devastated.

The confidence and future forward *we got this* thinking comes to an end the day *the voice* tells me he doesn't think he wants to get married.

The blood drains from my head. I feel faint. Shock consumes me again.

The words come out in a flurry,

"No! I can't believe you would do this to me. You infect me with a disease I will have for the rest of my life and now you tell me you don't want to be with me? Hell no!" Eventually, he changes his mind. Our wedding plans are back on.

There is no "right" or "wrong" way to experience shock. Typically, it's an initial reaction of which you are not in control. Someone else can't tell you what it's *supposed* to feel like, and you shouldn't judge yourself for experiencing it.

Even if you saw divorce coming or are the one who initiated your divorce, it doesn't mean you might not experience some degree of shock when it happens. It is one thing to intellectualize that something difficult and clearly life changing is about to happen; it's another thing when it is happening.

<u>Denial</u>

"This is not happening to me."

Let's not make this about semantics because it's more about the emotion behind it. Denial language can sound a lot like Shock language. One difference is that Shock generally has some physiological components that are abnormal. Heart rate changes and perspiring to name two. Denial can happen with none of those physical effects at play. Denial doesn't mean you've lost touch with reality. It means you're processing this new reality as best you can in the moment.

Denial, or disbelief, often follows so closely behind shock that they seem to overlap. Denial can show up as an unwillingness to accept that divorce is an option. It can also look like you are making efforts to save your marriage because you aren't willing or ready to believe it's over.

When you are in shock or denial, it's not a good time to make important decisions because there's a chance you're not in your rational mind and you have tuned out your intuition. Your survival instincts may have kicked in which means you are likely to take rash, *life-saving* actions, and no matter how horrible it feels, knowing you're getting a divorce is not a life-or-death situation.

Dealing with the reality of having herpes, my thoughts are all over the place. I'm in survival, *life-or-death* mode. Tina Lifford, author of *The Little Book of Big Lies* might tell me my surviving self (lowercase s) is on full alert. It's true that I am doubting my ability to cope, worrying about being alone, and resisting what the universe is trying to tell me: *This man is not your husband.*

The fact that I'm fighting to stay with someone who I no longer trust won't register with me for some time. When it does register, I realize it isn't about him. It is about the fact that I don't trust myself enough to realize I can deal with having herpes. I didn't have a choice about contracting it, but I do have a choice about how I live with it. And what

I know is that dealing with a sexually transmitted disease is better than the *dis-ease* of being with someone I don't trust. This is what Tina Lifford might recognize as my thriving Self (capital S).

Today, I can tap into calmness under pressure. All the emotions are there, and I don't deny that they exist, which is how I know I've gotten better at managing my emotions rather than being managed by them. It's difficult for someone else's behavior, intentional or otherwise, to send me spiraling to a place where I feel like I'm not equipped to deal with a situation.

5-4-3-2-1 Technique

Now is the perfect time to learn techniques that can help you when you're losing your emotional footing or experiencing the disconnect that comes from disbelief. This is a technique called the **5-4-3-2-1 Grounding Technique**. I like this technique because you feel immediate results.

Find a place where you can be still, preferably a quiet place. The first part is identifying **five** things you can see. Look at each thing and describe it to yourself. Notice the color, shape, and design. Does the texture look smooth or rough? Does the object look light or heavy?

Next, acknowledge **four** things you can touch. It can be a piece of your clothing or your hair. Maybe it's your chair, a table, or your cell phone. It doesn't matter what it is, as long as you can physically touch it. Again, consider how the item feels. Is it warm or cool to the touch? Is it soft or hard? Pliable or not?

Then, listen for **three** sounds. It can be your breathing, heartbeat, the air coming through a vent in the room, traffic, or voices in a nearby room. Now, acknowledge **two** things you can smell. And finally, **one** thing you can taste?

This grounding technique brings your focus back to what's going on around you. When your thoughts are all over the place, this exercise can ground you, so you feel more in control of yourself. I recommend that one of the **four** things you touch is yourself. Give yourself a huge hug during that part of the exercise.

Anger

Generally, I agree that there is no right or wrong way to experience these stages. However, in the case of anger, I would say that the wrong way would be any way that causes you or someone else harm. Or any way that is out of alignment with how you want to show up in the world.

Realize that anger can be a good thing. Where shock and denial typically lack focus, anger is generally targeted. That means you know you are angry with or at someone or about something. You might be angry with God, your spouse, your therapist, or yourself. It could even be displaced anger, and even that is directed, or misdirected, towards someone or something. What's important is that you acknowledge the anger and that you find a safe way to express it. Be honest and don't judge yourself for how you're feeling.

This will be challenging for you if you believe that expressing or acknowledging your anger is a sign of weakness, shows a lack of control, isn't feminine, or isn't God-like. If these things are true for you, it's possible you have conditioned yourself to suppress your anger or deny that it exists.

Stop the bullshigiddy! Anger is a primary emotion. Some psychologists say it is one of the primary emotions that are pre-wired into our brains. While there is debate about how many primary emotions there are, there is no debate over their existence. I'll share these six:

Anger: fury, outrage, wrath, irritability, hostility, resentment, and violence.

Sadness: grief, sorrow, gloom, melancholy, despair, loneliness, and depression.

Fear: anxiety, apprehension, nervousness, dread, fright, and panic.

Enjoyment: happiness, relief, bliss, delight, pride, thrill, and ecstasy.

Disgust: contempt, disdain, scorn, aversion, distaste, and revulsion.

Shame: guilt, embarrassment, chagrin, remorse, regret, and contrition.

Denying that you feel any of these emotions is counterproductive to your healing process. When it comes to anger, if you don't use it as an excuse to harm someone—emotionally, physically, or otherwise—there can be healing in addressing the emotion. Acknowledge that you're angry, and again, figure out what it's trying to teach you.

Consider asking yourself questions like:

- Why do I feel angry?
- What am I angry about?
- Who am I angry with?
- What did they do, or what happened?
- Why does it matter?
- What does it mean for me?
- What is the anxiety about?
- How would I rather feel at this moment?

You can't fix what you won't face, and you can't face your fear until you identify it. It's ok to be afraid. Now is a time you can empower yourself to explore the fear and find out why it's there.

If you truly want to challenge yourself, review the last question on that list and figure out if there's something you can do to get yourself to that emotional state. Don't bypass the other questions!

One more thought on the complexity of human emotion. It is said that grief is love with no place to go. This begs the question: Can we experience multiple emotions at the same time? The answer is yes. You may grieve the end of your relationship and still have love for your ex, while experiencing a sense of peace and freedom that an unhealthy relationship has ended. When this happens, it might be helpful to journal about your feelings. Identify the emotion. Then, identify what or to whom the feeling is associated.

Bargaining

On the brink of or during the divorce, you or your partner might say, for the first time ever,

"I know I never wanted to go before but I will do anything, including therapy, to make this work."

After the divorce you or your ex might think,

"If we had just gone to therapy, we could've saved our marriage."

These statements and others like them are what bargaining sounds like. Bargaining is what my grandmother called the "what if's." What if I do this, or what if I had done that? You imagine a series of scenarios and play them out in your mind to see if you can come up with a way that prevents what's happening from happening.

When bargaining happens near the end of a relationship, it is rare that the relationship can be salvaged. Last-ditch efforts are often futile. And unless both individuals make the decision to take extreme action to rebuild the relationship, it's likely going to end. When it does, the bargaining mind games that continue will be nothing more than your brain attempting to find a solution by creating an outcome that is no longer a realistic option.

Depression

As much as we want to avoid depression, it is as necessary a part of the grieving process as any other stage. The problem is—depression makes other people uncomfortable. People around you may want you to "Snap out of it," and "Cheer up!" because they don't like *seeing you like this*. Truth is, that may be more about their discomfort at feeling helpless than it is about you and what you need.

You are entitled to feel the sadness that comes from loss. You are allowed to be depressed. Sit with that for a minute. Literally, find a place and sit with it because what you're feeling is likely the thing that will ground you in the full reality of what is happening. You may have hit the proverbial rock bottom when you realize that your marriage or relationship is over. And that may be cause for deep sadness.

I love how Dr. Kubler-Ross explains it. She says, "Depression is a way for nature to keep us protected by shutting down the nervous system so that we can adapt to something we feel we cannot handle."[1] There is a real and necessary reason for depression. Not clinical depression that never lifts, but the depression that is a natural part of the grieving process.

Yes, if you're concerned that your depression has gone on too long, it is interfering with you being able to function day-to-day, or your thoughts are becoming destructive, then do see a doctor. I highly recommend therapy even if you aren't in the depression stage. In many instances, therapy is a mental wellness gift you give to yourself.

A good therapist can help you monitor your depression and recommend you to a doctor if they think it's warranted. Only a trained professional can determine whether medication might be helpful. At the same time, don't be alarmed if you feel depressed.

You can ask yourself questions like:

- Have I lost something or someone I once loved?

---

[1] Kubler-Ross, E., & Kessler, D., MD. (2014). *On Grief and Grieving*. Scribner. (Kubler-Ross, M.D. and Kellser 2005)(Original work published 2005)

- Am I missing something that was a huge part of my life or my identity?

- Do I have a right to be sad?

Answering these questions may help you realize that you have good reason to feel depressed. Once you accept that, give yourself permission to experience your depression, so it can serve its purpose and then leave.

Kubler-Ross suggests we treat depression like a visitor, even if it's an unwanted guest. She writes, "Allow the sadness and emptiness to cleanse you and help you explore your loss in its entirety. As you grow stronger, it may return from time to time, but that is how grief works."[2]

This made me think of the lyrics to Billie Holiday's song "Good Morning Heartache."

> Good morning heartache
> You old gloomy sight
> Good morning heartache
> Thought we said goodbye last night
> I tossed and turned until
> It seemed you had gone
> But here you are with the dawn
>
> Wish I'd forget you
> But you're here to stay
> It seems I met you
> When my love went away
> Now everyday I start by saying to you
> Good morning heartache, what's new
>
> Stop haunting me now
> Can't shake you no how

---

[2] Ibid.

Just leave me alone
I've got those Monday blues
Straight to Sunday blues

Good morning heartache
Here we go again
Good morning heartache
You're the one
Who knew me when
Might as well get use to you
Hanging around
Good morning heartache
Sit down[3]

It seems Billie Holiday had it right. Invite the heartache in. Sit with it. Feel everything. It's part of the process. Then, go take a walk, exercise, read a book, and dance with yourself. I'm not telling you to stop being depressed. I'm suggesting you continue to move, stretch your mind, and live through your depression.

As a child, my mother once gave me ten minutes to deal with being in a bad mood. I was an adult before I realized some people stay in bad moods indefinitely. Use that as an exercise for yourself. Set a timer for 3 to 5 minutes. This is the amount of time you will devote to experiencing the emotion. Setting the timer allows you to engage the emotion without it consuming you indefinitely. Once the timer goes off, sit the emotion down and get on with your day.

This bears repeating: Seek help if you can't move through the depression, if it feels like it is getting worse, or if you begin thinking of harming yourself or someone else.

---

[3] Billie Holiday, "Good Morning Heartache," January 22, 1946, Sony/ATV Music Publishing LLC.

Testing

Identifying the problem before you brainstorm for solutions seems obvious. If you've gone through depression, you've experienced the pain of your loss. Hopefully, you've had a good cleansing cry to purge some of the stress from your system. If you haven't gone through the depression stage, don't worry—it may come later. Remember this process isn't always linear.

Testing is when you consider ways of dealing with the loss you've experienced, so you can begin rebuilding your life. This can be a beautiful time in this Loss Cycle because it's a time of exploring options and asking questions. Because your brain will always work to answer whatever you ask it, be mindful of the questions you ask and how you ask them. Be specific.

Instead of asking: What's wrong with me?
Ask: How will I deal with this?
Or more specifically: How will I learn from this and find joy on the other side?

Write your questions down and read them back to yourself. It may take practice for you to learn to ask yourself the right questions, in the right way.

Acceptance

Your divorce is real. You know it's real. And you're ready to face the reality. In Acceptance, you acknowledge that your life is changing, and you consider how this is going to impact your life and other relationships.

I invite you to complete my *Review and Begin Anew Guide* located in Resources at www.divorceisnotadestination.com. Use the guide to review your relationship. Identify what you want for yourself moving forward. Reviewing with clarity, honesty, and acceptance is a gift because it allows you to process the loss with a focus on your future. When you arrive at the Acceptance stage, you will be more than ready to do this.

Rebuilding

Yes, this is stage number eight. Consider this a bonus stage. I've seen several lists representing loss associated with divorce. In one of the lists I reviewed, Dr. Jamie C. Williamson included Rebuilding. Rebuilding speaks to me because I see it as empowering behavior.

Rebuilding is when you are ready to let go of your past and move into designing your future. Again, it doesn't mean you won't have periods of feeling depressed or angry. You may cycle through any of the stages again, but you will do it from a different perspective when you are in the Rebuilding stage.

Empowering Reflections

Accountability means taking responsibility, even if you didn't cause whatever it is begging for your attention. Even if it goes back to your childhood. While you can't do anything about the past, you can seek to understand how it is impacting you today. Then, ask yourself: Is this what I want for myself?

When the answer is "no," you are positioned to change.

Clarity helps foster solutions that position you to embrace Accountability, so you know what to do next.

Part I

Put a check mark next to any of the stages you remember experiencing before, during, or after your breakup or divorce.

Then, circle the one that represents where you are today.

- Shock
- Denial
- Anger
- Bargaining
- Depression
- Testing
- Acceptance
- Rebuilding
- Abso-fricken-lutely tired!

Part II

If you identified where you are now, take ten minutes and write down how this stage manifests with you. For example, what does it look or feel like for you to be angry?

Then, look at the list and see if you can remember being in any of the other stages. Write down a sentence or two giving an example of when you were in each stage and how that felt.

The purpose of this exercise is for you to get tuned in to your emotions. Often, we try to avoid, ignore, or deny discomfort. That stops now. You are built to handle your life and that includes your emotions.

CHAPTER 3

When Grown Folk Talk

*"When we deny our stories, they define us. When we own
our stories, we get to write the ending."*

— BRENE' BROWN

"Marina, hold on."

I enter the kitchen and duck, lowering myself to clear the edge of the kitchen table. The table is round and only fits comfortably in our small square kitchen because it's pushed into the corner. One of the four chairs of the kitchenette set is the only thing preventing the table's edge from touching the wall.

Rising from her chair, always positioned under the telephone base mounted to the wall, is Nana. A lit cigarette goes from delicately balanced between her two fingers to her mouth. Placing it between the "mmm" shape her lips have made to hold, not inhale.

Instinctively, her left shoulder rises to meet her ear, trapping the yellow telephone receiver. Adjusting the coiled yellow phone cord out of her way begins our morning ritual.

With the phone and her cigarette now secure, Nana grips the table's edge with both hands, pulling it carefully away from the wall. The adjustment lets me wiggle my head and shoulders into the newly created space between the table and chair. Once seated, I'm positioned perfectly to eat, hear every conversation, and be in nobody's way.

Like millions of other families, our kitchen is the central point of our home. If the family Bible is on the kitchen table, it might be because Nana and one of my aunts are discussing or debating some Biblical text.

Conversations between Nana and Miss Marina or Miss Caroline happen daily. The topics range from what's going on at work, to family business, to gossip like who is having an affair, a baby, or a bad day. I know the gossiping is getting more serious when I hear Nana's voice fade to a whisper.

Adults talk about all sorts of things when they think a child is too young to understand or not paying attention. Around adults, I make myself scarce by lingering in hallways, hanging out on the stairs, and lying under the coffee table where I feel invisible, out of sight yet within earshot.

Being quiet and out of the way frees adults to discuss all manner of things. It is how I learn about Gampy's view on out-of-wedlock pregnancy and why my mother graduated from high school with two daughters and a husband.

Pregnant, Unwed, and Young

By the 1950s and 60s, almost 200 maternity homes for unwed mothers exist in the United States. Among them are the Florence Crittenton Homes. Initially serving as shelters for prostitutes, or "erring and wayward" women, they convert to maternity homes for unwed pregnant teens and young women.[4]

Author Ann Fessler, in her book, *The Girls Who Went Away*, interviews women representing the 1.5 million who surrendered their babies to adoption in the decades before Roe vs. Wade. Fessler's interviews reveal how fear and coercion play an enormous role.

Women are told their children will be bastards because they aren't married and that the best thing for the child is to be raised by married parents. One of her interviewees shared her thoughts at the time, "It may kill me to do this, but my baby is going to have what everybody keeps saying is best for him."[5]

The challenges don't end with forced adoption. Childless mothers return home to unite with their parents with well-rehearsed cover stories. For instance, pregnant residents could be found sunbathing on the rooftop at the Florence Crittenton Peoria Home in Peoria, Illinois. Their tans presented as evidence of their visit with friends in Arizona.[6]

It's important to point out three things: First, segregation is in full effect even within the walls of maternity homes, rendering the Florence Crittenton Homes and many other maternity facilities off-limits to pregnant teens and young women who happen to be Black.

Second, although there aren't nearly as many facilities and the resources aren't equitable, similar options exist for Black women and teens, like the Florence Home for Colored Girls in Kansas City and the St. Gerard Maternity Home in Virginia.

Third, a prevailing stereotype suggests that Black women and girls are promiscuous and "natural" mothers. The latter is a holdover from slavery when Black women were used to breed enslaved laborers. The

---

[4] (Spoerre 2021)
[5] (Fessler 2007)
[6] (Strickland 2015)

former contributes to the social stigma rooted in the idea that getting pregnant out of wedlock equates to promiscuity.

For my mother and grandparents, this increases the socialized and racialized shame experienced when my mother's pregnancy is revealed.

In the '60s, Lincoln Park isn't unlike many communities when it comes to pregnant teenagers. It is not uncommon for the girl to be sent out of state to family members or friends, where they give birth away from the prying eyes of the community. Their babies will be given away through an adoption process that may or may not be legal and raised by a friend, family member, or someone in the community.

Regardless of how embarrassing it is for Nana that her eldest daughter is pregnant at 15, abortion is out of the question on Gampy's watch. Sending mommy to live with family members out of town until she gives birth is also not an option to be entertained. Giving one of his children away, and we are all Gampy's children, is inconceivable.

The solution? Months before I am born, my parents marry in a small ceremony at Clinton AME Zion Church in Lincoln Park.

Not at Our Kitchen Table

Of all the things adults talk about at our kitchen table, I don't recall discussions about divorce. For that matter, neither do I recall discussions about deep love, all the reasons marriage should happen, and how to ensure the marriage lasts. Maybe these conversations happen late in the evening or before I make it to my chair in the morning. Perhaps Nana is a better whisperer than I realize.

Then again, in the 60s, getting a divorce is not only taboo but a sure path to poverty for many women. That being the reality, perhaps the prevailing thought in our kitchen and many others is, *what is there to talk about?*

Marriages in our family don't seem to be of the romantic variety. They aren't steeped in sugary sweet gestures and fairytale-themed beginnings. Recently, I was on a long drive with my mother and her sister Nadine. My mother is the eldest of five. Nadine is the second oldest and less than a year younger than my mom. Both were pregnant in their teens. My mother had me at sixteen, and if my calculations are correct, Nadine was seventeen when she became pregnant with my cousin Stacey. Taking advantage of having them trapped in my car for 5-½ hours, I ask questions.

"Would either of you have gotten married if you weren't pregnant?

My mother responds first. Quickly and almost defensively, "I loved Billy."

Something in her response makes me smile. Perhaps because it's good to hear that your parents were in love. Also, while I know she truly loved Perry, she maintained some affection for Billy.

Still, I dig deeper. "But would you have married him if you weren't pregnant?"

"No," she answers, "I wouldn't have married him at sixteen."

I ask Nadine, "Would you have married Joe Pop if you hadn't been pregnant?"

"No." There's no follow-up. That is the complete sentence.

Less than 24 hours later, I call my aunt Dariece, who also gets married after learning she is pregnant.

Her answer to the same question is an emphatic "No!"

My mother and two of her four sisters marry after getting pregnant. The other two get pregnant out of wedlock and don't marry. One refuses to identify the father. The other involves a young man who isn't interested in getting married. Kitchen table conversation reports two motivations for getting married. One is likely to get out of their parent's home. The second reason is they are pregnant during a time when pregnancy is a liability for women.

Signs of the Time

Each Magruder girl has their first child between 1962 and 1975. Before 1974, a woman can't get a credit card, open a checking account, or get a loan or a mortgage unless a man, her father or husband, co-sign. It doesn't matter if she earns more money than him or if she is the one paying the bills.

The birth control pill is legalized for use by unmarried women in 1972. The system is not designed for women to be self-sufficient and independent or live like equal partners in their marriages. Ultimately, my mother and her sisters make the best decisions, given the circumstances. Resulting in marriages that have little to do with partnerships based on respect, mutual appreciation, and the alignment of values. A perfect foundation for discord leading to divorce is baked into these relationships.

By the time I marry for the first time, I'm aware of nearly twenty divorces in my immediate and extended family. And I can tell you almost all the components leading up to and planning a wedding and nothing about how to potentially avoid divorce or how someone can care for themselves when facing the traumatic experience of going through one.

Collateral Damage

Today, I know that breakups and divorces often result in aftershocks that cause fractures in relationships beyond the two people getting divorced. Referred to as "friendship fallout" or "collateral damage," it's when relationships between in-laws, friends, and acquaintances dissolve as people feel they must choose sides.

It's a reminder that divorce is not exclusive to marriage. The "friendship fallout" or "collateral damage" can occur whenever we separate ourselves from a person, place, or situation.

---

di·vorce (noun)

the legal dissolution of a marriage by a court or other competent body.

- legally dissolve one's marriage with (someone).

- separate or dissociate (something) from something else.

Divorcing From a Toxic Environment

"My father was not a nice man."

Whenever Nana speaks about her father, she reminds me he was not nice.

When Nana is nine, her mother dies in the basement of a hospital in Bethesda, Maryland because *Colored* patients aren't allowed on the main floor. Her death leaves Nana and her brother Charles in the care of their father, who was not a nice man.

The first time I hear the words "cat o' nine tails" is from Nana as she describes what her father used to beat her. A cat o' nine tails is a multi-tailed whip. The nine tails, made of strips of cotton or rawhide, are often knotted to inflict more pain. It was designed as an instrument of punishment used by the Royal Navy, the British Army, and the judicial punishment system in Britain and other countries. This is what Nana's father used to beat her.

"Sometimes, I would try to hide under the bed. My father would drag me out from under the bed and just whip me."

When she tells this story, Nana's lips draw tight together like she's still trying not to cry from the beating. Through clenched teeth she tells me,

"I didn't want to give him the satisfaction of knowing how much pain he was causing me."

What makes the beatings more painful is the fact that she often doesn't know why she is being whipped.

A few years after her mother dies, Nana's father takes her brother Charles, leaving her to live alone in the house. During that time, there is one neighbor who checks on her periodically.

"Why didn't the neighbor take you home with her?" I ask.

"She had a house full of children and was barely making ends meet."

For money, Nana collects glass soda bottles and returns them to get the deposit money. It's only a few cents per bottle, but every penny she gets counts.

In addition to high school and figuring out how to get from day to day on her own, Nana's father demands that she do his cleaning jobs. Some of the people in the community hired him to clean their businesses. Nana cleans the businesses and turns the money over to her father. Before her high school graduation, Nana figures out a way to divorce herself from this situation.

The vision that keeps her motivated is a family gathering in New Jersey. One summer, her father takes Nana and her brother Charles to visit Cousin Inez. Cousin Inez lives in South Jersey and works as a sewing instructor at a school for girls. She also sews costumes for entertainers working in the clubs in Atlantic City.

Nana always smiles when she says, "This is the first time I remember thinking, this must be what a family is supposed to be like."

Something takes hold of Nana during this visit that changes the possibilities she sees for herself. It becomes the impetus for creative thinking that changes the trajectory of Nana's life.

Expect Your Plan to Work

"My father is raising his cleaning service prices by 5 cents."

This is what Nana tells the owners of the businesses she has been cleaning for her father. She makes everyone aware of the price increase except her father. The client pays the increase, and Nana pays her father what she always pays him. The extra nickel she sets aside for herself. By the time graduation comes around, Nana has enough money to buy herself a cardboard suitcase.

"It didn't occur to me that I didn't have enough clothes to justify buying a suitcase."

This part of the story always makes me laugh. Partly because Nana always laughs when she tells it. Mostly because I try to imagine a suitcase made from the cardboard boxes Gampy brings home from the grocery store that I use to build tents in the basement.

The point is that Nana has a plan that she fully expects to work.

The plan is to attend her high school graduation ceremony, get her diploma, and make her way to the bus station. All she needs to do is make it to that bus station, and she will be on her way to Cousin Inez in New Jersey. No more beatings. No more collecting soda bottles. No more having to fend for herself. Cousin Inez represents family, and Nana is all too ready to find out what it feels like to have a real one.

Plans Change - Deal with It

"You're too stupid to graduate!"

The words ring in her ears. In an instant, her father ruins her escape plan. It is one thing to be a poor Black girl running away to another state. What she is not going to do is be a poor Black girl with no proof of having graduated high school, running away to another state.

Too stupid to graduate. Listening to her tell these stories, I conclude that my grandmother was a pretty smart kid. At least she was smart enough to figure out how to earn enough money to buy a suitcase and a bus ticket without her father finding out. As young as I am, I'm fully aware that there are many words that could be used to describe Margaret (Pinkett) Magruder, and stupid is not one of them. Not now. Not then. Not ever.

No matter what he said, she did earn that diploma. Missing her graduation ceremony is upsetting, but she focuses on what she can do. Her intention is clear. Her objective is to get her diploma, even if the plan on how she will do it must change.

A few days later, Nana visits the school in hopes of getting her diploma. Success! With her nearly empty cardboard suitcase in tow, her next stop is the bus station. There, she boards a bus that carries her to Cousin Inez and a fresh start in New Jersey.

These stories reveal Nana's intellect, problem-solving skills, and how and why she developed her stern, no-nonsense demeanor. In all fairness, her childhood didn't leave much opportunity for her to be a child. She had to figure things out for herself, by herself. When she became a mother, she had to learn on the job.

Aspirations, Objectives, and Goals

Before I continue with Nana's story, I want to provide definitions for words so you will know what they mean to me as you continue reading. The words are Aspirations, Objectives, and Goals. Objective and goal are often used interchangeably when in fact, they are different. My definition is heavily influenced by my coaching from Myron Golden and the fact that, well, the definitions are different.

Aspirations – Ambitions or long-term visions of what you want to achieve. They become the foundation for your goals.

Goals – Broad high-level endpoints you aim to achieve that align with your aspirations. This is the pot of gold at the end of the rainbow.

Objectives – Specific, measurable steps or targets that support achieving your goals. If you think S.M.A.R.T. Goals should be called S.M.A.R.T. Objectives, I agree.

Let's use Nana as an example. Nana's aspiration was to be free of the abuse and position herself to experience what having a real family felt like. Her goal was to get to Cousin Inez's home in New Jersey. The many objectives or steps she took to achieve the goal that would make her aspiration a reality were:

- Raising her father's fees and saving the nickels
- Purchasing a cardboard suitcase
- Picking up her high school diploma
- Catching the bus to New Jersey

It's safe to say that your aspiration will be most powerful when it is connected to something emotionally significant. The value you place on the aspiration is what gives meaning to each step along the way.

Now, back to Nana's story.

<u>You Do Better When You Know Better</u>

"I felt great when I was pregnant."

Nana loved being pregnant. Unfortunately, she is clueless when my mother, their firstborn arrives. One day, my mother will not stop crying. The crying goes on for what feels like hours. Nana tries everything she can think of and is near tears from frustration and exhaustion. When a neighbor stops by, Nana tells her,

"I've tried everything. I've fed, changed, bathed, and walked her around. This child will not stop crying."

The neighbor picks my mother up, places her over her shoulder, and pats my mom firmly on her tiny back. My mother lets out a loud, long burp! She turns to Nana,

"It's a wonder the child didn't blow up. She was full of gas, Margaret." She hands my mother back to Nana.

Nana is too relieved to be embarrassed.

When you know better, you do better, is a line Nana says often. So often that I am an adult before I realize it is a Maya Angelou quote, not a Nana-ism. Nana embodied that quote. She firmly believed and instilled in me that I could learn anything.

By the time Nana dies, we are all appreciative of the fact that while her sternness wasn't always easy to receive, we are thankful for what it instilled in us. We know the difference between being victimized and being victims and Henry and Margaret's children are not victims. We are who we are mainly because of the woman she was. There's much to learn from the people who raised, loved, mentored, and nurtured us.

Hopefully, sharing my family story encourages you to discover more about your own. Learn from a place of love. And know that while one incident or segment of time won't tell the entire story, one incident can profoundly impact future events. Finally, resist the urge to judge anyone's past.

Unspoken: A Lineage of Divorce

There is no way for me to write a book entitled *Divorce Is Not A Destination* without examining the history of divorce in my family. So, here it goes.

Relationship	Number of Divorces
Mother	1
Father Billy	2
Father Charles (Perry)	2*
Grandfather Summerour	1
Grandmother Summerour	2
Aunt Dariece	2*
Aunt Jean	1
Aunt Nadine	1
Aunt Roberta	2
Uncle Charles	2
Uncle Perry	1
Sister Peggy	1
Sister Tami	1
Niece Renee	1
Niece Chanelle	1
Brother Charles	2
Cousin April	1
Cousin Desi	1
Cousin Daryl	3
Cousin Leticia	1
Cousin Robert	1
Cousin Shannon	1
Me	4

*Indicates that either a legal marriage or divorce may not have taken place. However, the relationship was or is treated as if a marriage did occur.

By the time I marry for the first time, I am aware of nearly twenty divorces in my immediate family. Examine your family stories and create your list.

If you come from a family where divorces are rare or non-existent, questions that surface for you might include:

- What do I believe about people who get divorced?

- Do I feel negatively judged for getting divorced? Either by others or by myself?

- Do I have support?

- Do I feel isolated?

- How do I feel about myself?

For a way to process your breakup or divorce experience, use my Breakup and Divorce Review to Begin Anew worksheet. Find it under Resources at www.divorceisnotadestination.com.

Empowering Reflection

What conversations about relationships do you recall hearing adults discuss when you were a child?

- Marriages
- Friendship
- Divorces
- Affairs
- Adoption (legal or otherwise)

- Love
- Dating
- Pregnancy
- Abortion

Do you recall anyone explaining to you what divorce is?

CHAPTER 4

A.A.C.T. In Joy!

*"Freeing yourself was one thing, claiming ownership of that
freed self was another."*

— TONI MORRISON

"The devil is a liar!" Bonita scuffed.

Bonita and I are sitting close enough to have a conversation that no
one else is paying attention to because they are equally engrossed in
their own chats.

Nearly a dozen of us are sitting in a cluster like high school kids in the
cafeteria. Adjusting chairs to get closer as we speak in whispers. When
necessary, we sync our head nods and burst into laughter at another
memory from more than thirty years ago. Anyone who has ever
attended a funeral is familiar with the much-needed laughter that comes
after the *we're sure gonna miss you* tears.

As Bonita speaks, I notice what hasn't changed. Her dimples remain in
full effect, and her disposition is as light and welcoming as ever. She
tells me how her son was labeled learning disabled, and she was told he
would need to be placed in a special program at school. She was having
none of it.

"Yes, the devil IS a liar," she repeats.

As only a mother could, Bonita took matters into her own hands and opened a daycare, where she did everything she felt the school system wasn't going to do for her son. Today, he's a college graduate with a wonderful career.

"But girl, I've been married a few times."

When you've been married multiple times, conversations about divorce can be exhausting. Part of you is on alert, preparing for judgement, criticism, unwarranted comments, and unanswerable questions. But there is something in the way Bonita transitions to, *but girl, I've been married a few times*, that feels different. So, I welcome the invitation to *go there*.

"Bonita," I lean in, "you know I was an overachiever in high school."

Our eyes meet, brows arching in unison.

"How many times have you been married?" I ask.

"Three." She waits to see if I will match her number.

I hold up four fingers.

Her eyes twinkle. We laugh loud enough to draw attention.

Gathering ourselves, we quiet down. In my gut, I believe Bonita knows every bit of shame, guilt, and insecurity I've experienced through the years concerning my divorces. The next question I ask is sincere and borne out of a genuine desire to know.

"How do you deal with the comments when people find out you've been married and divorced multiple times?"

The expression on her face tells me two things. She's familiar with the comments to which I'm referring. And I am about to hear a quotable.

"Oh, I just tell them it's because I'm the marrying kind."

This gives me life! I beam at how she takes an often-asked question and the negative connotations attached to it and flips it into a testament to desirability and attractiveness. Bonita shifts the narrative and offers me another perspective. One that doesn't associate multiple marriages with being damaged, damned, desperate, or defective.

If I never utter the words, "I'm the marrying kind," out loud, they will still resonate in me whenever conversation around multiple marriages begins. The ability to flip the script can be just what you need to fuel an emotional adjustment. What script do you need to flip so you can see yourself in a more becoming light? Don't be defined by life's experiences. Define yourself based upon how you decide to show up in your life.

Nearly 50% of the marriages in the United States end in divorce, and the likelihood of divorce increases with each subsequent marriage. Bonita and I are in that latter category. We would also categorize ourselves as having been in high-profile positions. It is important to me that individuals whose marriages don't make it to *'til death do us part* have support, resources, and community.

Recalling Bonita's story and examining my own experiences, I'm aware of the similarities in our lives. Causing me to wonder, how many others might relate and be helped if I could answer the question, "How did you get through it?"

Pop Quiz

Has your breakup or divorce kept you from:

1. Dreaming big

2. Pursuing your dreams

3. Achieving objectives

4. Making positive changes in your life

5. Getting out of bed

Accountability, Alignment, Communication, and Trust (A.A.C.T.) In Joy!

Choosing to A.A.C.T. In Joy! will be one of your most challenging yet rewarding experiences. Life changes are not for the faint of heart. It is for you if you are ready to do the inner work necessary to exact the change you desire to have the quality of life you know exists. Fully engaging in the A.A.C.T. In Joy! process is a gift you give to yourself.

The acronym A.A.C.T. represents a proprietary multi-step process to empowered living. For many, this process is how they will rebuild their confidence. For others, this is how they will learn to relieve themselves from the frustration of trying to control their environment and the people in it, focusing on the one person they can control—themselves.

It's likely that you're learning about the A.A.C.T. In Joy! process because of your unique issues surrounding a breakup or divorce experience. You will find that it works equally as well with other relationships, including those in your professional life.

A – Embrace **Accountability** by taking responsibility for those things within your purview.

- Assess
- Act With Intention
- Cultivate a Growth Mindset
- Track Your Progress

A – Create **Alignment** between your values, what you value, and how you show up in the world.

Divorce Is Not A Destination®

- Awaken Your Values
- Aspirations and Objectives
- Consider Your Purpose
- Train Your Brain

C – Communicate clearly and without guilt.

- Assertive Expression
- Active Listening Skills
- Clear and Concise Messaging
- Talk to Yourself First

T – Learn to **Trust** yourself and you will grow to trust others.

- Affirm Self-Trust
- Attain Post-Traumatic Growth
- Connect to Self
- Transformative Mindset

"In Joy!" is more than a catchphrase. Even the "in" has power. It is a preposition. It indicates a state or condition of joyfulness within the framework of Accountability, Alignment, Communication, and Trust. Making joy more than a separate or external element. Joy is intricately woven into the fabric of these principles.

Including "in" is both an implication and an invitation to experience joy as an integral part of your engagement with Accountability, Alignment, Communication, and Trust. It signifies a holistic and positive approach, emphasizing that these elements are not just tasks to be completed but opportunities for personal and collective fulfillment and joy.

Joy is often used interchangeably with happiness. For me, joy is a deeper, more enduring state not dependent on external factors. This internal contentment generates gratitude, inner peace, or connection beyond oneself. Through a combination of mindset, perspective, and intentional practice, joy can even emerge when facing difficult situations.

Nobel Prize winner, Archbishop Desmond Tutu put it this way, "Joy is much bigger than happiness. While happiness is often seen as being dependent on external circumstances, joy is not."

A.A.C.T. In Joy! is an inner-view process that empowers you to address circumstances with clarity and confidence. A.A.C.T. In Joy! doesn't get you to a destination in as much as it provides a vehicle that informs and enriches the journey. Because once you can cultivate inner joy, you will realize—it's the key to living a wonderful life.

Heal Thyself

Ultimately, the objective is to lead your best physical, mental, emotional, and spiritual self forward. This requires that you engage intentionally when it comes to caring for yourself. For the most part, there are two primary paths to wellness. The conventional practices associated with Western medicine, and the philosophies and methodologies associated with Eastern healing practices.

Fortunately, there is an increased recognition of the complementary aspects of Eastern and Western medicine. Integrated medicine combines the strengths of both approaches, emphasizing a holistic understanding of health and wellness. Before I provide details on A.A.C.T. In Joy! I will share a few alternative healing practices you might want to research and explore.

Alternative Healing Practices

Whether you use natural medicine or holistic healing, it's good to familiarize yourself with other practices that aim to promote overall well-being and balance. Consider that there may be benefits in combining healing modalities. Below is a list of some common holistic healing practices you might consider learning more about, if they aren't already familiar to you.

Acupuncture - Involves the insertion of thin needles into specific points on the body to stimulate energy flow and promote balance. It is often used in traditional Chinese medicine.

Ayurveda - An ancient system of medicine from India that focuses on balancing the body's energies (doshas) through diet, herbal remedies, yoga, and lifestyle practices.

Chiropractic Care - Manipulation of the spine to address misalignments and improve the functioning of the nervous system, promoting overall health.

Energy Healing - Various practices, such as Reiki and Qigong, involve manipulating or channeling energy to restore balance and promote healing.

Herbal Medicine - The use of plants and plant extracts for medicinal purposes to address physical, mental, and emotional imbalances.

Homeopathy - A system of alternative medicine that uses highly diluted substances to stimulate the body's self-healing mechanisms.

Meditation - Mindfulness and meditation practices, including techniques like guided meditation, transcendental meditation, and mindfulness-based stress reduction, to promote mental and emotional well-being.

Naturopathy - An approach that emphasizes the body's ability to heal itself using natural remedies, including herbal medicine, nutritional counseling, and lifestyle changes.

Nutritional Therapy - Focuses on using a balanced and personalized diet to promote optimal health and address specific health concerns.

Reflexology - Massage and manipulation of specific points on the hands, feet, or ears, believed to correspond to different organs and systems in the body.

Sound Therapy - The use of sound, such as singing bowls, gongs, or music, to promote relaxation, reduce stress, and enhance overall well-being.

Tai Chi and Qigong - Mind-body practices that combine gentle physical movements, breath control, and meditation to promote balance and energy flow.

Yoga - A holistic practice that combines physical postures, breath control, meditation, and ethical principles to promote overall well-being.

Crystal Healing - Using crystals and gemstones to balance energy and promote healing, often aligned with the chakra system.

Aromatherapy - The use of essential oils extracted from plants to promote physical, emotional, and mental well-being through inhalation or topical application.

Prayer - A way for individuals to express thoughts, emotions, gratitude, requests, or supplications to a deity, higher power, or the divine. Prayer can take various forms, including spoken or written words, silent contemplation, meditation, or ritualistic actions.

Breathwork - Breathwork or breathing exercises, techniques, and practices that involve conscious control and manipulation of breathing patterns. The primary focus of breathwork is on using your breathing as a tool for self-regulation, relaxation, and personal growth.

It's important to note that while many people find holistic healing practices beneficial, individual results and responses to them can vary. When warranted, you should consult with your primary care physician or therapist for serious health concerns and to inform them of any complementary or alternative therapies or practices being considered.

Be safe. Do your research. And keep in mind the possibility of combining conventional and holistic practices with a well-balanced diet.

Take A.A.C.T.ion

At the beginning of this chapter, I introduced you to Bonita. What Bonita does masterfully is ask herself the right questions. Bonita doesn't ask what childcare services, schools, teaching staff, or social service programs can do for her son. Instead, she asks herself, *What can I do?* Then, she set out to get it done.

After taking in the information provided, Bonita determines that the outcome prescribed to her is not acceptable. Bonita takes **Accountability.** Then she lives and acts in **Alignment** with her faith, her belief in her ability, and her desired outcomes for her child. She identifies the resources she needs and **Communicates** her needs to those who can support her. Bonita would no doubt tell you that she trusted in God first. I will tell you that Bonita also needed to **Trust** in herself.

A.A.C.T. in Accountability

When you've been treated poorly in a relationship and don't feel you've done anything wrong, it can be difficult to consider holding yourself accountable. Trust the process and allow yourself to experiment with the idea because it will bless you. Empower yourself by taking ownership of a past situation that is impacting your present-day—negatively. When you get the hang of this, how the situation came to pass will be irrelevant. This is not a power play; it's an empowered play! Here are four areas that make up the A.A.C.T. of Accountability.

Assess

Think of Assessing as taking inventory by reflecting on past decisions and actions related to your breakup or divorce. Let me share something

I learned from a colleague, even if you believe your ex was responsible for 99% of the problems in your relationship that leaves you with 1%. Your assignment is to commit to taking responsibility for 100% of that 1%!

The objective is to determine why you made the decisions you made, not punish yourself for having made them. This is not about undoing the past; it is about learning from what your past reveals to you and about you.

Implement the assessment process at any time. Use it to dissect past decisions that are still weighing on you or to help you determine the best decision to make concerning a current situation.

- Can you identify specific decisions or actions related to your breakup or divorce that still weigh on you?

- How do you feel about reflecting on your past decisions without punishing yourself?

- In what ways do you think assessing past decisions can contribute to your personal growth?

Act With Intention

Intention is when the reason for taking the next step is aligned with your objectives. One way to honor your intention is to consider the desired outcome. In the case of your breakup or divorce, do you want to be able to engage in civil conversations with your ex? Is your desire to create a healthy co-parenting environment? Do you need to establish or reestablish boundaries to protect your emotional well-being? Are you at a point where you want to embrace new possibilities for yourself by shedding behaviors that no longer serve you or those around you?

Identifying your objective will help you set the behavior required to achieve it. Think of it like the captain of a boat. My father had a sailboat For several years. Sailors understand that although they chart a course to a specific destination, the wind and current are constantly taking the vessel off course. Their job isn't to sail a straight line; it's to continuously guide the boat back on course toward the destination.

Set your intention and move toward your outcome. Be flexible and trust that you can handle situations that may take you off course. If you do find yourself off course, don't pass judgement. Redirect.

- What are your objectives related to your breakup or divorce? Consider aspects like communication with your ex, co-parenting, setting boundaries, and personal growth.

- Can you think of intentional behaviors that align with your desired outcomes in these areas?

- How can you remain flexible while staying committed to your intentions?

Cultivate a Growth Mindset

The concept of a growth mindset was developed by psychologist Carol Dweck. You can read about it in her book, *Mindset: The New Psychology of Success*. A growth mindset refers to the belief that one's abilities, intelligence, and talents can be developed and improved over time through dedication, effort, and learning.

Individuals with a growth mindset embrace challenges, see failures as opportunities for growth, and persist in the face of setbacks. They view setbacks and obstacles as temporary hurdles rather than fixed limitations, and they actively seek out opportunities to learn and expand their skills. This mindset fosters resilience, perseverance, and a positive attitude toward learning and personal development. In contrast, a fixed mindset is characterized by the belief that abilities and intelligence are innate traits that cannot be changed, leading individuals to avoid challenges and feel defeated by failure.

Cultivating a growth mindset will benefit you in all aspects of your life.

A growth mindset empowers you to believe in and anticipate your ability to overcome hardships, heartache, and other challenges in ways that strengthen your resolve and fortify your resilience. Seeking knowledge and adapting to change reinforces the connection between growth and accountability.

- Reflect on instances where you have demonstrated a growth mindset in the past. How did it impact your resilience and ability to overcome challenges?

- In the past, how comfortable have you been with continuous learning and adapting to change? If you answered, "not very", you aren't alone. And today is the day you can decide to be and do differently.

- Are there specific areas in your life, apart from the breakup, where cultivating a growth mindset could be beneficial? If so, what are they?

Track Progress and Celebrate Successes

A fourth component of Accountability is tracking progress and celebrating. There is something magnificent about watching children. In fact, watching adults with children can reveal what seems to be an innate ability to track and celebrate the smallest things. Birthday parties are a way of tracking age progression. How about the markings on the door frame used to track growth spurts—did your parents do that with you? What about you with your child?

And as far as celebrating small successes goes, I bet you don't clap and cheer for yourself when you finish your vegetables or go to the bathroom. But you've probably done it or looked on supportively when it's been done by another adult who was celebrating a child's accomplishments.

As adults, we often get too busy to make time to celebrate our small successes, wins, or achievements. Change that today. Moving forward, give yourself permission to track your progress. Here's an easy start. Hanging on the wall in my office is a large self-adhesive post-it pad. It is where I track the books I read each year. This simple win makes me smile and is in alignment with me being a life-long learner.

The beautiful thing is I get to celebrate it with others. It's almost guaranteed when my friends Curtis and Vanetta visit, he is going to want to see my current reading list. That reading list regularly becomes my gift list and reading recommendations for clients.

Tracking your progress will foster a sense of accomplishment and motivation, reinforcing your commitment to personal growth and accountability. This is how you can weave a narrative of self-empowerment, resilience, and a proactive approach to shaping a fulfilling life beyond divorce.

- What small successes, wins, or achievements related to your breakup or personal growth can you acknowledge and celebrate?

- How do you currently track your progress in different areas of your life?

- Can you think of one way to track and celebrate a success, no matter how small, and make a conscious effort to celebrate it regularly?

Accountability Exercise

Create a Personal Growth and Accountability Journal:

- Set up a dedicated journal or use an existing one.

- Divide it into four sections, one for each component of **A.A.C.T. in Accountability** (Assess, Act with Intention,

Cultivate a Growth Mindset, and Track Progress and Celebrate Successes).

- Write your reflections, objectives, intentional behaviors, growth mindset exercises, and celebrations in each corresponding section consistently.

- Review your journal periodically to track your progress and reinforce your commitment to personal growth and accountability.

Before you move on to Alignment, find a way to celebrate what you've just completed.

A.A.C.T. In Alignment

Awaken to Your Values

Every day we make judgement calls of what's right and wrong based upon what's important to us. Values influence what we think and how we feel. And often, our values inform how we behave. Values are an intrinsic part of what we see as meaningful.

Values are not constant. They can change throughout our lifetime. Going through a divorce means you've experienced significant change in your life. This is a great time for self-rediscovery and a reassessment to determine what's important to you now.

Self-rediscovery can be an exciting journey that provides an opportunity to explore your passions and interests. Consider what activities no longer serve you and whether you've neglected any passions during your previous relationship. Awakening to your values is key to the process of acknowledging and aligning them with your life.

As you embark on this transformative journey towards a more fulfilling life post-divorce, you have the freedom to design your roadmap to self-rediscovery and empowerment."

- Make a list of three aspects of your life that you want to explore in this phase of self-rediscovery.

- How has your identity been shaped by past experiences?

- What aspects of yourself would you like to redefine moving forward?

- Visit www.divorceisnotadestination/resources to access a Value Assessment tool.

Aspirations and Objectives

What to do with the new you? The time will come for you to define and refine your Aspirations and Objectives. Document the things you learn about yourself as you identify what you value today. Spend time thinking about where you see yourself in one, three, and five years. Take it to ten years even. How will you challenge yourself to move in the direction you've set for yourself?

Consider creating a vision board to vividly illustrate the life you desire post-divorce. A vision board prompts you to craft a tangible representation of your aspirations, serving as a constant reminder of the link between your daily actions and the vision you have for your future.

Thinking back decades, to my days as a high school athlete, I use visualization techniques regularly before each event. Before an event, I visualize executing perfectly. When I miss in my visualization, and sometimes I do, I continue to visualize it until I get it right. In my mind's eye, I see myself approaching, taking off and clearing the high bar, leaving the blocks, and smoothly running through the first three hurdles, or launching myself into the long jump pit without scratching. As a teenager, I have no understanding of the neuroscience behind what I'm doing; I just believe it works.

If you've never created a vision board, I highly recommend that you do. In 2012, I create a vision board using personal photos, magazine ads, decorative sheets, and old pieces of art paper from my days with Creative Memories. It's colorful, and it has been hanging in my home office for more than ten years.

A message on my vision board reads, "My corner office has a great view." And it does; both at home and from countries around the world.

About two years ago, I'm sitting in the living room looking out the window at our palm trees, sunlight beaming in from windows on two adjacent walls. Then it hits me: this is my vision board in real life. Everything depicted on my vision board has come to pass. There I am earning my doctorate degree, getting paid as a speaker, instructor, facilitator, coach, and author—all while running a business from home. Sometimes, I even work from cruise ships and in exotic locations while vacationing with family and friends. I'm also great at tacking on mini getaways to the beginning or end of business trips, which continues to be part of my vision. You can visit resources at www.divorceisnotadestination.com to see my 2012 vision board.

How you accomplish your Aspirations and Objectives will depend on you identifying them and preparing yourself for the journey. Creating a vision board alone won't bring aspirations or objectives into existence. Instead, it serves as a creative expression of your desired objectives.

In her book, *The Source: The Secrets of the Universe, the Science of the Brain*, neuroscientist Dr. Tara Swarts discusses the science behind visualization and the power of creating what she calls an action board— her version of a vision board. It's important to understand that expecting a favorable outcome and preparing yourself for that outcome must be part of your vision board process.

- Create or update a vision board for your aspirations and objectives for the next one to five years.

- Reflect on your long-term objectives. Identify challenges and steps you can take to prepare yourself for achieving your objectives.

- Immerse yourself in your vision! Use sensory visualization techniques. This is where you envision yourself in the setting: What activities will you participate in? How will it feel, smell, sound, and look when you are there?

Consider Your Purpose

In the aftermath of a breakup or divorce, identifying your purpose will be a transformative and integral component of your personal growth. Identifying your purpose is an introspective journey that requires reflecting on your core values, passions, life experiences, skills, and aspirations. It is not a static destination but a dynamic process that unfolds over time, shaping your decisions and actions.

Purpose serves as the guiding force that infuses meaning into your life. It is the reason you wake up in the morning, offering clarity, direction, and a profound sense of fulfillment. Beyond a mere objective, purpose reflects your authentic self and the impact you wish to make on the world.

Defining or clarifying your purpose after a breakup or divorce a pivotal moment.

In the self-discovery journey, purpose shapes your legacy. It's not just about impacting others; it's a testament to living authentically. Purpose guides you toward a

About Your Authentic Self

This is your internal compass, and you must be aware of it before you can learn to redirect yourself back to it when you do go off course. And life is designed that you will get off course.

When you do; acknowledge that it happened and realign with what's important. That's keeping it real.

post-divorce life filled with intention, resilience, and connection to your true self, empowering growth and embracing a future rich with meaning and fulfillment.

Enjoy addressing the following:

- Think of a difficult experience in your life and write down what you learned about yourself because of it.

- What are you passionate about?

- What do you love to do?

- Who do you love to help and why? *Who are you a hero to?*

- What are you naturally good at?

- If money weren't an issue, what would you dedicate your time and energy to?

Train Your Brain for Alignment

There's no question there will be times when you are distracted and drawn off course. When this happens, your ability to realign will be crucial. Remember the boat captain who is constantly checking their instruments and countering the elements to put the vessel back on course over and over.

If your breakup or divorce feels like a storm, you now have information that can act as your beacon to see you through rough times. Awakening to your values, identifying your aspirations and objectives, and considering your purpose are markers along your journey to help you stay the course.

- What mindset shifts are necessary for you to embrace change as a natural part of your divorce journey?

Divorce Is Not A Destination®

- Write two or three sentences that include your values, aspirations, objectives, and your purpose that reflects how you want to show up in the world.

Alignment Exercise

- Recall a challenging experience in your life, particularly one related to your breakup or divorce.

- Recall a challenging experience in your life, unrelated to your breakup or divorce.

- Write down what you learned about yourself going through these difficult periods. Consider how the experiences shaped or reshaped your values, aspirations, and understanding of your purpose.

A.A.C.T. In Communication

Assertive Expression

This is about you—prioritizing your needs and emotions through a "Me First" approach. It's not selfish; it's self-compassion in action.

When you name your emotions, do so with kindness. Avoid judging, hiding, or downplaying how you feel. This is about empowering yourself to embrace and express your thoughts, feelings, and needs. It's a source of personal strength, a way to be without compromising your boundaries.

Assertive communication is more than just a tool; it's a game-changer. Once you set boundaries, maintaining them requires clear communication, especially when they are challenged. This approach becomes your ticket to navigating the complexities of post-divorce life with newfound confidence and resilience. It's not about erasing challenges; it's about facing them head-on, tapping into a strength you may not have known was within you.

Are you ready to embrace assertive expression and redefine how you navigate life after divorce?

- Reflect on a recent situation where you found it challenging to express your thoughts or needs. How might adopting a "Me First" approach and practicing assertive expression have changed the dynamics?

- Why is it important to establish and maintain healthy personal boundaries in post-divorce life? How can assertive communication contribute to this?

Active Listening Skills

Active listening skills are essential in shaping your post-divorce communication dynamics. It's not just about hearing words and giving instant responses; it's about truly understanding and connecting with others. These skills lay the groundwork for building meaningful connections. There are practical exercises to make these skills a part of your communication toolkit.

As difficult as this may be with your ex, if it is necessary for you to maintain communication with them, it will benefit you to have the capacity to reflect on what they are communicating. This isn't just a strategy; it's a powerful tool that will enhance the quality of your interactions with your ex and others.

To navigate post-divorce communication with your ex, you'll need empathy, understanding, and a commitment to constructive engagement. Engagement is tied to your psychological and emotional commitment, fueled by your values, which enable you to invest in a relationship, often despite the other person's state of mind or behavior.

When it comes to engagement, one question you can ask yourself at any point is: How is what I'm about to say or do likely to improve or enhance the other person's engagement? Yes, you might be hurting, disgusted, and annoyed to new heights and I'm asking you to step outside yourself and think about the other person. Given the circumstances, this may be one of the most challenging things for you to consider and I'm asking you to consider it anyway.

Why? Because while you may feel like you're doing something for them that they don't deserve; the truth is, your behavior is about you. It's about how you've decided you want to show up in the world. It's about your growth. It's about being accountable to yourself.

Taking the time to read this book and learning to do something different is a start. Learning something new is great. Putting it into practice is the objective. Knowledge that isn't practiced is just a good idea.

Embracing accountability and honoring your values make engagement easier, as you're guided by your internal compass rather than external factors, such as someone else's behavior. Mind you, I'm not suggesting that you tolerate abusive behavior. Instead, I challenge you to refrain from labeling *annoying* behavior as *abusive* to give yourself permission to disengage.

Ready to equip yourself with more skills for your journey?

- List behaviors that have annoyed you in the past and visualize yourself not being distracted by them. Or visualize how boundary setting can help you navigate or negate annoying behaviors, so you can focus on effective, mutually beneficial communication.

- Practice active listening in your next conversation. Summarize what the other person says to you and validate their emotions. Notice the impact on the quality of your communication.

- How can active listening improve your comprehension and increase your empathy in post-divorce communication?

- Why is reflective communication valuable in building meaningful connections? Reflective communication is when you summarize what the person said to be sure you understand it from their perspective. You do this instead of responding immediately with your thoughts or comments.

Clear and Concise Messaging

Navigating healthy communication post-divorce can feel like walking through a maze with no guide. Communicating with an ex often takes a turn for the worse during and after the divorce. When communication is necessary, using clear and concise messaging can decrease tension, lessen the amount of time you need to be in communication, and hopefully, expedite resolutions. And, as you learned in the previous section, focusing on engagement can help.

Every word you speak holds the power to shape your interactions and relationships. Avoid using vague or ambiguous language that can lead to confusion. Taking the time to write down what you want to communicate in advance will be time well spent. Stay on topic to avoid dredging up past issues or creating unnecessary discord.

Open body language means being as physically relaxed as possible. Avoid crossing your arms or frowning when communicating with your ex. Pay attention and work to relax areas in your body that feel tense. These pointers should be adhered to when you're in person and when you're having a telephone conversation.

Your voice has a different tone when you're smiling, and smiling causes your body to release dopamine and endorphins known to boost your mood. No matter how silly you might feel, commit to doing it. Revisit your values, objectives, and purpose to help you realign your thinking about this if you're struggling with it. Ask yourself which behavior reflects the person you are growing into. The one who can smile through the bullshigiddy? Or the one who allows themselves to be sucked in by someone else's old behavior patterns?

And remember, it's a process. Don't beat yourself up if, or when, you get triggered and fall back into an old pattern. As time passes, you will go from reflecting on these moments after they happen, to stopping yourself as they're happening, to catching yourself before you react. With practice, there will come a day when you see the behavior that once triggered you for what it is. None of your business!

With practice, you will learn to navigate conversations with your ex concisely, clearly, and confidently. It's time to reclaim your voice and steer your interactions toward brighter outcomes.

- Write down a recent communication where there was a misunderstanding. How could you have framed your message more clearly and concisely?

- In what way does non-verbal communication play a role in your interactions?

- In the past, what were ways you and your ex used non-verbal actions to communicate negative thoughts and feelings?

- How can heightened awareness of both verbal and non-verbal cues improve your ability to communicate? Be specific.

- What do you need to stop doing?

Talk to Yourself First

This exploration emphasizes the importance of engaging in honest conversations with your inner self. It's not about comfort; initiating change may feel uncomfortable in the beginning. This introspective journey is crucial for aligning your values and purpose and a little discomfort won't hurt you. Before expressing your thoughts outward, get clear internally. Ensure that you are being honest with yourself so you can establish a solid foundation.

Building upon the principles in Accountability and Alignment, "Talk to Yourself First" is the bedrock of fostering open, honest communication. It invites you to explore your passions, recognize your strengths, and envision aspirations within the framework of your values. Talking to yourself first is a guide, illuminating the path to a deeper self-awareness which will enhance the clarity you bring to your external communications.

- How might engaging in honest self-dialogue contribute to your understanding of your own insecurities and doubts?
- How might engaging in honest self-dialogue contribute to your understanding of your own wants and needs?
- How might this inner dialogue help you make the connection between why your insecurities and doubts are preventing you from moving toward your wants and needs?

Communication Exercise

- Select one of the four areas under Communicate—Assertive Expression, Active Listening, Clear and Concise Messaging, and Talk to Yourself First. Write about how using it will benefit your current communication style.

A.A.C.T. In Trust

Affirm Self-Trust

It's time for you to look at what makes you amazing. Take a moment to recognize and affirm your personal strengths. Building trust in yourself is key, and in this journey, you'll uncover the deep connection between acknowledging your strengths and building resilience. Here are a series of exercises to guide you toward affirming self-trust.

Reflect on Past Achievements: Write a list of past successes and accomplishments, both big and small. Remind yourself of moments when you trusted your instincts and made positive decisions. This reflection can reinforce your belief in your abilities and resilience.

Practice Self-Compassion: Be kind to yourself and acknowledge that going through a divorce is stressful. Treat yourself with the same compassion and understanding that you would offer to a friend in a similar situation. Recognize that it's okay to make mistakes. Learn from them and make them part of your growth process.

Set Boundaries: Establish clear boundaries in your relationships and daily life to protect your well-being and honor your values and needs. Saying no when necessary and advocating for yourself can help you regain a sense of control and autonomy. And yes, you can say "no" with a smile.

Strengthen Your Intuition Muscle: At some time in my teens, mother started encouraging me to *listen to my gut*. On Mel Robbins; podcast, *The #1 Neuroscientist: After Listening to This, Your Brain Will Not Be the Same*, Dr. Tara Swart shares a three-step process to help you make, what I believe will be value-based decisions because they come from your gut. The process involves tapping into your intuition:

- Rest your forehead in your hands and ask, *Is this what I really want?* Take five deep breaths.
- Place your hands on your chest over your heart and ask yourself emotionally, *Is this what I really want?* Take five deep breaths.
- Put your hands on your stomach and ask intuitively, *Do I really want this?* listen for your response.

Seek Support: Surround yourself with supportive friends, family members, a therapist, or a breakup and divorce coach who can offer encouragement and validation. Having a strong support system can provide reassurance and perspective during challenging times. Review information on creating a Support Team in #2 of Chapter 6.

Celebrate Personal Growth: Recognize and celebrate the progress you've made on your journey of healing and self-discovery. Celebrate your resilience, courage, and newfound independence as you embrace this new chapter of your life. If you are reading this book, that is one thing you can celebrate.

Journal what comes up for you and review it. You might realize that you want a clean house, but you dislike cleaning. Consider hiring a cleaning service. Perhaps you love the work that you do, but you don't care for the people you work with? Is it time to switch departments, explore new job opportunities, or start your own business? Maybe you've remained in a difficult or toxic relationship because you have anxiety about giving up your current lifestyle and making it on your own. Use this exercise to listen to yourself and gain clarity.

- **Objective Setting Inquiry:** Consider an objective you've set for yourself post-divorce. How will achieving this objective reinforce self-trust?

Attain Post-Traumatic Growth

Many find the journey to self-trust after a breakup or divorce to be the most difficult. Ironically, it has also proven to be the most liberating part of the growth process. Peeling away layers of doubt and apprehension that have accumulated over the years can be rejuvenating.

Developing resilience is about your ability to bounce back when faced with adversity or significant life changes. Resilient people cope effectively with stress, overcome setbacks, and maintain a sense of psychological well-being. After an emotionally distressing experience, being resilient allows you to recover relatively quickly and function effectively. Resilience is about adapting positively.

Post-traumatic growth goes a step further. It refers to the positive psychological changes that can occur when you overcome adversity.

Instead of bouncing back to your pre-adversity state, when you experience post-traumatic growth, you transform. This could mean gaining a greater appreciation for life, developing new perspectives and priorities, experiencing enhanced personal strength and resilience, deepening relationships, and finding new meaning or purpose in life.

Post-traumatic growth is about acknowledging the scars left by the divorce while simultaneously recognizing the seeds of strength that have taken root in the fertile soil of adversity. This journey toward growth isn't about erasing the past; it's about transforming its lessons into catalysts for personal empowerment. Think of it as a pilgrimage toward the core of your being, where authenticity and self-trust become the cornerstones of a reimagined future. More than moving forward—it's growing forward.

- **Inner Resilience Exploration:** Reflect on a challenging phase during your divorce. How can acknowledging what you've already endured and overcome serve as a starting point for your journey toward post-traumatic growth?
- **Scar and Strength Acknowledgment:** Write about a scar left by the divorce that you recognize and identify a strength that has emerged from that experience.

Connect to Self

Before making healthy connections with others, secure your connection with Self. And remember, *yes, I'm going to say it again*, it's a process. Whatever you do, don't spend time nurturing relationships with others to avoid looking in the mirror and saying to yourself, *I love you. I trust you.*

It's my belief that we can set ourselves up for disappointment and others for failure when we depend on affirmation and validation from outside ourselves. Because as soon as that external source isn't capable or available to feed that need in us, we fall apart. If you want to develop secure, healthy relationships with others, establish a secure and healthy relationship with Self.

One of the most important things you can do for yourself when it comes to trust is something my mother started telling me when I was a teen: trust your gut. To do that, take a moment and ask yourself, *how do I feel?* In any given moment, slow down and tune into what your body is experiencing. Challenge what you've been told and connect to your inner voice.

In 2019, I lost a mentor and dear friend, Mrs. JoAnna LaSane. Mrs. LaSane was a contemporary and colleague of my grandmother. Whenever I would call her, struggling with what to do, she would say,

"Be still. The answer is inside you. Be still and listen."

Tuning into this will support you in developing that your intuition muscle and alert you to how often you second-guess yourself. You will realize how often you ignore what you're feeling to go along with what someone else is thinking you ought to do.

Master this, and you will change your life immeasurably. Steven Bartlett is an investor, entrepreneur, and host of the #1 podcast in Europe, *The Diary of a CEO*. When it comes to making decisions he says, "Perfect decisions only exist in hindsight."

If you are a recovering perfectionist like me, you may have learned that perfectionism breeds procrastination. And I firmly believe that procrastination disguised as contemplation will result in stagnation. Make decisions for yourself that feel right—i.e., they are in alignment with what's important to you. Trust that you have the tools to deal with the outcome, no matter what it may be, and move on.

Two areas where many often hesitate to be honest with themselves or speak up are in intimate relationships and at work. To get good at making healthy decisions, you must trust yourself to make them.

- If your current relationship is unhealthy and not working, honor yourself by saying something to your partner. You will either position the two of you to work on it, or you will realize it's a relationship that needs to come to an end.

- If you're at a job where you feel devalued, underappreciated, and overworked, honor yourself by saying something to your boss. Conduct job searches to learn about other opportunities. Knowing what's out there is empowering. And if nothing changes, you've begun prepping to leave if leaving is what's best for you.

Connecting more deeply with Self will ultimately help you forge more authentic relationships in every area of your life because you will have embodied authenticity. The people attracted to you will be individuals who appreciate, admire, and respect how you show up when you trust yourself first.

- **Feel the Disconnect:** Think of something you are currently doing that does not feel right for you. Ask yourself:

  o Why are you doing it?

  o What is keeping you from doing something different that aligns with what you know to be best for you?

- **Genuine Connection Visualization:** Envision a genuine connection you would like to build post-divorce. How can this connection be a source of trust in your interpersonal interactions? Do you represent the aspects of this connection you find attractive?

Transformative Mindset

Developing your trust muscle will strengthen your empowering mindset. The ability to trust yourself is often diminished during a difficult relationship. That means healing and growth after a breakup or divorce hinge on you trusting yourself.

It begins with a shift in mindset that acknowledges past experiences but refuses to let them define the future. And it includes intentional behaviors that reflect the new way of thinking and being. Instead of dwelling on feelings of betrayal or inadequacy, embracing a transformative mindset involves recognizing the power of personal agency.

Transforming your mindset works when you take accountability by reframing past challenges as opportunities for learning and empowerment. Believing that every setback is a steppingstone toward greater self-awareness and inner strength is how you will get there.

Everything you've covered in *Divorce is Not a Destination* up until now, has led you to this point. Acknowledge that your emotions and experiences are valid. Do so without judging yourself. Recognize that vulnerability is not a sign of weakness but a testament to your courage. By cultivating self-awareness and practicing self-care, you can rebuild a sense of trust in your own intuition and abilities.

Does this mean that every carefully thought-out decision you make will work out? No, it doesn't. It means that you trust yourself enough to know that you can handle yourself either way. Trusting in your ability to make healthy decisions is important. Believing that you are equipped to handle whatever challenges your life presents may be even more important.

It is often the anxiety we create from believing something will not work out that prevents us from making any decision at all. Don't live by default based on an imaginary negative outcome. Ultimately, even if you make no decision, *that* becomes your decision.

Learning to trust others again requires a similar mindset shift, rooted in forgiveness, empathy, and a willingness to be vulnerable. Because trust has been broken in the past, doesn't mean that all future relationships are destined to follow the same pattern.

By approaching new relationships with a willingness to communicate openly and honestly, you create space for authentic connections to flourish. This involves setting healthy boundaries, expressing your needs and concerns assertively, and being receptive to feedback from others. And disconnecting when you realize the relationship is not a healthy one for you to pursue.

Remember that it's okay to take things one step at a time and to seek support from trusted friends, family members, or professionals along the way. Trust is a journey, not a destination, and with patience, perseverance, and a transformative mindset, you can cultivate deeper connections and a renewed self-confidence after divorce.

- Reflect on an experience where you trusted yourself and it led to a positive outcome. What lessons can you draw from that experience to reinforce your decision to trust in yourself moving forward?

- Identify one area of your life you would like to build more trust in yourself. What small, actionable steps can you take to nurture that trust?

Trust Exercise

- **Make the Decision:** As you go through the next few days or weeks, pay attention to how often you make decisions for yourself and how often you ask for someone else's advice.

- **Be Your BFF:** The one person who will be with you forEVER is you. So be your best friend forever.

    o   Keep your own secrets.

    o   Be mindful that you aren't telling everything to impress people or to secretly get their approval.

o   Be as compassionate and thoughtful to yourself as you
     would be to your closest friend.

CHAPTER 5

Children and Change

"Divorce is not the end of the world. It's worse to stay in an unhealthy marriage. That's a worse example for the children."

— JERRY HALL

"Two Shirley Temples for the girls. And ask Charles if he can add extra cherries."

My eyes light up at the extra cherry request my mom made for our drinks.

It is Sunday afternoon and that means it is matinee day at the Wonder Gardens. The Wonder Gardens is a jazz and R&B club and one of the only Black-owned clubs in Atlantic City, New Jersey in the late 60s early 70s.

"Here you go."

The waitress sits our Shirley Temples down, and the bartender, Charles, didn't disappoint. Me and my sister Tami each have two cherries instead of one.

I touch the drink and feel the coolness. My fingers leave prints where they wipe condensation from the ice-filled glass. Our Shirley Temples are pinkish red, fruity, and have just the right amount of sweet and sour. Mr. Charles makes them look so good. He puts in an umbrella that sits on top of what looks like an extra-long toothpick. Above the umbrella sit two maraschino cherries.

The first cherry is eaten immediately. The second one I save until I finish the drink. The real test is the taste. One sweet sip followed by a mouth-puckering tartness, and Mr. Charles has done it again.

Mommy is in nursing school. She waitresses at the Wonder Gardens on the weekends. Some acts who perform there include Willie BoBo, The Delphonics, Harold Melvin and the Blue Notes, Kool and the Gang, George Benson, and B.B. King, who would eventually become part owner. One night, a group of five guys perform. Mommy found out they were hungry and needed someplace to stay that night. She brought all five of them to Nana and Gampy's house.

We woke up to Gampy barking, "Damnit! This girl got all these people here sleeping on my floor!"

Then, Gampy went into the kitchen and fixed them breakfast like they were family. Most of the time, Gampy's bark came with no bite. The five guys are straight out of college and just starting to get touring gigs. They call themselves the Commodores.

The matinees at the Wonder Gardens are special. I look forward to them because it's time with our mom. With her working and attending nursing school, time with her is precious.

Now, Mommy is dating Perry, and our regular matinee Sundays at the Wonder Gardens aren't happening.

And more change is coming.

Another Move

Mommy is parked in the lot at Farmington Elementary School. That means I don't have to take the bus home today.

I'm barely in the car when I say, "Guess what we did today?"

Mommy smiles. She knows I love school. I love that I'm in class with my best friend, Olivia. I love that I get to sit next to Joey. He has jet black, short, straight hair, cut like Moe's from the Three Stooges. Except Joey is cute. And he can make his teeth pop out like Gampy does at night when he puts them in a cup of water with something that fizzes and bubbles like an Alka Seltzer tablet. I think that is so cool. I imagine Joey does that with his teeth at night too.

"Mommy, today we used the green paper with the lines on it to practice writing our names in cursive. Mrs. Tan said I did a really good job."

As I reach into my bag to pull out the soft green paper with my name written in cursive, I ask, "Where are we going?"

Mommy doesn't usually pick me up from school. I normally take the school bus that drops me off right in front of the big house. So many people are going to school from our address; it is officially a bus stop.

"We're going to Perry's place," she answered.

Looking around the car again, I think, *this is a lot of stuff for a sleepover.*

Mommy and Perry have been dating for a couple of years. Today is the day Mommy has decided it is time for them to get serious. Them getting serious means me, her, and Tami are moving again.

We arrive at the little cottage in Pleasantville where Perry lives. Mommy calls him at work.

"Hi buka," her nickname for him. "I'm at your place."

"Oh, ok. I'll see you when I get off," he replies.

Mommy, wanting to be sure he understands this is not a visit, says, "Me and the girls are here moving in today."

"I'll be right home!"

Mommy hangs up the phone and begins unpacking.

Through a Child's Eyes

To say my and Perry's relationship got off to a bad start is putting it mildly. More than once, I imagine him getting hit by a school bus in front of my grandparents' home.

I think, *My mother will be sad, but she'll get over it.*

In my mind, Perry has given me many reasons to dislike him. I wonder if there is an emotion stronger than hate. First, he ruins my matinee Sundays at the Wonder Gardens. Now, he is taking me away from my grandparents, my best friend, and my school.

How will I ever find out what Joey does with his teeth at night!?

At nine years old, I don't know that the distance between the big house and the cottage is only seven miles. I just know it's a new school in a different neighborhood. That's all I need to know to hate everything about it.

At nine, it just feels like another divorce from everything I've come to know.

A short time later, when Mommy asks if we want to change our last name to Perry after they marry, I muster up all the nine-year-old energy possible to tell her, "No!" Fortunately, my mother honors my wish, and our last name remains Summerour.

Where the Heck is Milwaukee?

In the summer of 1974, we load up the car for a road trip and family vacation. It's fifteen hours to Milwaukee, where we will stay with

Perry's brother Alvin, his wife Evie, and their daughter Shannon.

We aren't there long before Aunt Evie is on a campaign to get my parents to relocate. And my mother seems all too interested.

It took two weeks for Aunt Evie to sell my mother on the benefits of raising a family in the Midwest. Before we drive back to New Jersey, Mommy has a job offer from St. Mary's Hospital, my parents borrow money to put down on their first home, and my dad is applying for jobs and planning on attending grad school at UWM.

We move into our house at 3033 N. Newhall St. in August of 1974. Tami and I walk to Bartlett Elementary School, less than two blocks away. Kevin begins his sophomore year at Riverside High School, also two blocks away from our home.

As you can imagine, I wasn't thrilled about this monumental relocation either. And you can guess who I blamed.

Breakup Conversations with Your Child

Having grown up as a child of divorced parents and then becoming a stepchild, I am compelled to share with those of you who have children; your child is experiencing everything you are experiencing during your divorce in some way. And children don't benefit from processing the experience with a fully developed brain.

It could be detrimental to your child's well-being to assume that because of their age, they don't understand what's happening, aren't as impacted by the changes, and don't need support. These changes can be more emotionally impactful on children because they are feeling things they don't understand and aren't always able to verbalize. Emotional discord is worse if the child feels they aren't allowed to verbalize their feelings because no one has given them the time or space to do so.

If you're going through a break-up or divorce and your heart is aching, being vulnerable and honest with your child is crucial. Your objective is to do everything possible to establish and maintain a healthy relationship with your child. Here are some things to consider:

Age-Appropriate Information: All information you share with your child should be age-appropriate. Now is not the time to make your child your new best friend. Even if your child is mature for their age, they are still a child, and there is likely information they do not need to know. Tailor the information you share taking into consideration their age and maturity level. Provide simple explanations without oversharing or creating confusion.

Open Communication: Initiate an open, honest, and age-appropriate conversation with your child. Choose a time and place where you can talk without distractions. Encourage them to express their feelings and thoughts. Let them know that you will always make time to listen and speak with them.

Express Emotions: Be vulnerable by sharing your emotions with your child. It's perfectly fine for you to acknowledge the pain and sadness you're experiencing. Be mindful not to burden them with too much detail. Avoid blaming the other parent. More on that later.

Reassurance: Reassure them that the break-up is not their fault. Emphasize your love for them and your commitment to being there for them.

Maintain Stability: Do everything possible to maintain routines or create new ones. Routines provide stability and demonstrate that despite the changes, there are things they can count on. This could be dinner at a certain time each night at the dinner table, a bedtime routine, or Saturday movie matinees. Emphasize your commitment to co-parenting and how even though you aren't together physically, you will work together as parents.

Encourage Questions: Invite them to ask questions and express their concerns. Be patient and ready to provide answers, even if those answers involve acknowledging uncertainty. You do not have to have the answers to everything because you probably won't. "I don't know" is an acceptable answer when it's true.

Seek Professional Support: Consult a family therapist or counselor. Having a counselor who works with children available for you to speak with might be all you need. One of my clients had a teen who did not want to go to counseling. My client could speak with the counselor, share what was happening with her child, and be reassured that all seemed normal given the circumstances. You don't have to do this alone.

Avoid Negative Talk: Refrain from speaking negatively about your ex in front of your child. This is one of the things I respect about my mother. She never spoke negatively about our biological dad. And she didn't allow others to speak poorly of him around us either. Keep discussions focused on feelings and actions rather than blaming the person.

Be Prepared for Reactions: Understand that your child may react with various emotions, including sadness, anger, confusion, or withdrawal. Be patient and supportive. Let them express themselves without judgement. Refer to the Loss Cycle and see if you can identify what stage your child is in. If they are old enough, you might share that information with them and let them know their emotions are normal.

Model Healthy Coping Mechanisms: Children learn what they see lived. The more consistently you model healthy ways to cope with stress and sadness, the better your child will be at doing the same. Provide ways for them to express their feelings. It could be through art, writing, or talking to a trusted family member or friend.

<u>Dating Conversations with Your Child</u>

Whether you can't imagine dating right now, or you're ready to join a dating site *yesterday*, this section is worth the read. This information may sound familiar after reading about how to talk with your child about your breakup or divorce. For convenience, I will risk repeating information so it's easier for you to find later.

Initiate the Conversation: Find an appropriate time to talk, ensuring there are no distractions. Let them know you want to have a conversation about something important. Sometimes it's great to have these conversations in a place away from home. Know that you do not have to wait until you meet someone to have this conversation. Having the "at some point I will start dating" conversation before you meet someone may be less stressful for both of you. It could also create time for your child to get mentally and emotionally prepared in advance of the "I have someone I want you to meet" conversation.

Acknowledge Feelings: Recognize that your child may have a variety of emotions about you dating. Encourage them to share their feelings and reassure them that their emotions are valid.

Assure Them of Your Love: Make it clear that your decision to date doesn't diminish your love for them.

Explain Your Need for Companionship: Share that you seek companionship and connection. Explain that dating is a personal decision that doesn't change your role as their parent.

Introduce the Idea Gradually: Consider introducing the idea gradually rather than springing it on them suddenly. Share that you've been thinking about meeting new people and exploring the possibility of a new relationship.

Discuss Boundaries: Talk about any potential changes in routines or living arrangements that might come with a new relationship. Discuss how these changes might affect your child and establish boundaries that help them deal with discomfort.

Divorce Is Not A Destination®

Be Open to Questions: Invite your child to ask questions and express their concerns. Be prepared to answer honestly while respecting their age and maturity level.

Highlight Positive Aspects: Share positive aspects of introducing a new person into your life, such as the potential for new friendships and positive role models.

Emphasize Communication: Encourage ongoing communication between you and your child. Let them know they can always come to you with their thoughts or concerns. Remember, you cannot force your child to like someone just because you do.

Reassure Them with Stability: The best way to do this is by maintaining the routines you already have with your child. When that isn't possible, and if the new relationship is the reason, do all you can to establish a new routine in its place. Demonstrate to your child that they are a priority. Don't just speak about it, be about it.

If you have more than one child, remember that every child is unique. These tips may need adjusting based on their ages, personality, and past experiences. The key is to create an atmosphere of trust, understanding, and ongoing communication.

<u>Love Finds a Way</u>

First name? "Lisa."

Last name? "Summerour-Perry."

This is how I complete the registration form for the 1986 Miss New Jersey USA Pageant. Perry's full name is Charles Fulton Perry. Nana is the only person who knows that I've hyphenated his last name with mine.

Certain I will not win; I'm not concerned about the legality of changing my name on the pageant entry form. I'm only doing it to publicly acknowledge my love, respect, and admiration for Perry. After all these years, the decision to use his name is 100% mine. I'm hoping he feels the meaning behind that.

My parents' marriage isn't perfect. I've heard the arguments. I've learned of the infidelity. Still, their relationship represents the possibilities of what a marriage can be.

What their marriage proves to me is how divorce can be a pathway to a fulfilling future. Through their marriage, I learn that happiness can exist without perfection. Children can adapt to change. And a group of strangers can come together to form a family. It is difficult for me to type biological father and stepdad. But for the purposes of not confusing you, the reader, I've done it in this book.

Whether we choose the change, or it's thrust upon us by the adults in our lives, embracing change can make all the difference. We can be blessed, and change can bless us. When the change isn't of our choosing, it requires us having enough faith to believe good exists. It's the *seek and ye shall find* method of finding that one good thing.

I created The What Went Well? journals for adults and children so people can spend a little time each day reminding themselves of the good that happens around them and because of them daily. You can learn more about the journals at www.drlisasummerour.com.

Lessons From My Mother

"Your mother did practically everything wrong, and everything worked out."

This is something my godfather, Larry James Avery says to me during one of his visits. He's right. There is no scenario, where graduating high school with two children and a husband is desirable. And that was my mother's story. Well, part of her story. Fortunately, that isn't all of my mother's story.

Let's agree that there is no foolproof solution to eliminating the pain your child might experience during your divorce journey. So, that cannot be your objective. What works for one family might not work for yours. Matter of fact, what works for one of your children might not work for another. What you can do is acknowledge each child's individuality, share information, be willing to ask and answer questions, and listen. And avoid telling your child how they *should* feel.

Even with the less than desirable start, my mother does many things well. Things that make a profound difference in the relationship I grow to have with my biological father, Billy.

Bad-mouthing Billy in front of us doesn't happen. She never allows anyone else to speak negatively about him in front of us either. I have no idea if she threatens family and friends or makes them promise to keep his name out of their mouths, but disparaging comments about him never make it to the kitchen table when I'm around.

Another thing she does is make sure he has access to us and that he knows how to reach us. It is never about where he is or what he's doing or not doing. Seeing us is not part of a reward program where the rules of access are constantly changing. Even when it causes her extreme anxiety to let us travel from Milwaukee to North Carolina to stay with him one Christmas, she puts on a brave face and off we go. Mind you, there is no court order and no joint custody in place requiring her to do anything.

When she started dating Perry, she made it a point to drive us to Rockville, Maryland and introduce Perry to Billy's family. Maintaining our connection to the Summerour side of our family is one of my greatest pleasures. It's unfortunate that so many children of divorced parents grow up disconnected from one side of their family because the parents are estranged. Knowing both sides of my family enriched my life.

My parent's teenage years were interrupted by parenthood and marriage. No more football for him or track and choir for her. It took my mother an extra year to graduate from high school.

By the time she meets and marries Perry, my mom is only twenty-three. Getting pregnant makes you a parent. Getting married makes you a spouse. Neither results in immediate maturity nor a spike in one's emotional intelligence. Be intentional about growing from wherever you are.

Empowering Reflection

Think of one good thing that came from your divorce, separation, breakup, termination, or relocation—you get the idea.

You may need to sit with it for a few minutes. It's not unusual that the first thought is, "Nothing good has come of it because it was a horrible experience."

If that was your first thought, ask yourself this question: If something good could come of it, what might it be?

It doesn't have to be something big. Just come up with one good thing. Write it down.

Chapter 6

Seven Things to Help You Right Now

If your heart is aching, it's not broken. A broken heart is one that has stopped feeling anything.

— Dr. Lisa Summerour

Christine's number is blinking on my caller ID. Excited; I answer immediately.

"Hellooo! How are the wedding plans coming along?"

"I'm divorcing Trent," Christine responds. "Can you help me find an attorney?

Wait. What? Divorcing Trent? I don't understand.

Confusion strikes me like ice water spraying from my phone. How was she divorcing Trent? They weren't married.

Months before, I attended Christine's amazing bridal party weekend. It was planned to perfection by a group of her friends, and I anticipated her wedding being equally as fabulous. I answer Christine's call ready to share my thoughts on bridesmaid gown colors, invitation designs, and all things destination wedding related.

Christine is in her late thirties. She's a successful media professional working in one of the top markets in the United States. It's a high profile, high-pressure, moderately well-paying position that she navigates in award-winning fashion. Christine and Trent were being practical when they decided to elope several months before.

The wedding ceremony is nearly a year out. They are planning to start a family soon after marrying, and eloping meant Christine could be added to Trent's insurance plan now rather than waiting until later. What difference will one year make?

Shortly before Trent returns home from his last overseas tour, Christine receives a call from a woman in Korea.

"I want to talk with you about your fiancé," says the voice on the other end.

Christine declines to engage in a conversation with a stranger who she feels is just trying to start some mess. She ends the call.

Not long after, Christine receives text messages and photographs. In the United States, what she receives would be considered pornographic and possibly illegal. For Christine, these images are undeniable proof that Trent was involved in an adulterous affair. And whoever this woman was, she was not shy about sending every piece of evidence she had, and she had plenty.

That is how Christine, a woman planning her wedding, comes to needing a divorce attorney.

In his book, *I Just Want This Done: How Smart, Successful People Get Divorced Without Losing Their Kids, Money, and Minds*, Attorney Palmer Raiford Dalton talks about two kinds of emotional and sexual affairs.

The second type is an affair committed by a serial cheater who is unlikely to change. Dalton describes this person as someone who shouldn't be married. My mother would say that a man having an affair weeks after eloping shouldn't be married either.

No child has ever played dress-up and fantasized about the day they will get divorced. It's not a surprise that we are ill-equipped and unprepared when faced with having to navigate through one. This is also why going to therapy or finding a breakup and divorce coach may not be the first thing on your mind when faced with divorce.

There are so many other things that need your attention at a time when your attention span has been snapped! This chapter is here as an immediate "go to" to get you on the path to stability and alignment even though you feel like you're on a roller coaster with no end in sight.

#1. Name Your Feelings

You may have already noticed feeling out of sorts. Maybe you identify it as feeling like you're on an emotional roller coaster or drowning in emotions. Others may say you're having mood swings. If this sounds familiar, there is nothing wrong with you. Feelings of denial, anger, bargaining, depression, and acceptance are all part of the Loss Cycle (See Chapter 2).

Write down what you are feeling and identify where you think you are in the cycle. Here are three important things to know:

- People experience the Loss Cycle stages differently.

- The stages don't necessarily happen in a particular order.

- There is no specific time frame for how long you might stay in one stage.

- You might experience a stage more than once.

Note: No stage should last indefinitely. And be aware of depression. If it goes on for many months, seems to get worse, or you have thoughts of harming yourself or someone else —seek help immediately.

Identifying where you are in the cycle is powerful because it provides clarity about what's going on with you emotionally. Once you identify an emotional state, you can position yourself to use tools to control it rather than allowing your emotions to determine your behavior.

#2. Create Your Support Team

You don't need to have all the answers, and you won't. If you have been the "go to" person for everyone else, now is a time when you may feel helpless. Put your ego and pride aside and bless someone in your life by allowing them to support you. "It is better to give than to receive" only works when someone is willing to receive.

Consider including the following people in your support team:

- Legal advisor
- Financial advisor
- Fitness coach or partner
- A supportive friend or family member
- Your physician
- A breakup/divorce coach

As a person who has had more than one incredible therapist, I like to share the benefits of seeing a therapist or licensed counselor. I am a coach. While there can be overlap, there are differences between what coaches and therapists provide for their clients.

Coaches primarily work on a specific area, like in my case divorce. And coaches are looking at moving you from where you are, the present, to where you want to go, your future. Therapists are more likely to spend time helping you delve into your past to identify the root cause of ongoing issues. Therapists typically have a degree and are licensed. Whereas a coach may or may not be certified or accredited. The important thing is for you to do your homework and select someone who will be supportive, while still challenging you to do the necessary work.

If a child is involved, consider getting a therapist who specializes in working with children impacted by divorce. If you are struggling to deal with the changes happening in your life and see the benefit of having professional support, it's safe to assume that your child/children could benefit from professional support as well.

What's important is that you have a support team, and you take advantage of them by leaning on them when necessary.

#3. Get Your Stuff Together, Literally

Whether it's a divorce, separation, or something you can't name right now, this is a great time to get your stuff together—literally. Your support team will be instrumental in guiding you through this process. Ask the professionals! Here are a few ideas to get you started:

Financial Records:
Income statements (pay stubs, W-2s, tax returns)
Bank statements
Investment account statements
Retirement account statements
Real estate documents (mortgage statements, property deeds)
Loan documents (car loans, personal loans)
Credit card statements

Asset and Liability Documentation:
Inventory of assets (real estate, vehicles, valuable possessions)
Documentation of debts and liabilities
Business ownership documents (if applicable)

Expense Records:
Monthly budget
Documentation of regular expenses (utilities, insurance, groceries)

Legal Documents:
Pre-nuptial or post-nuptial agreements (if applicable)

Any existing court orders or legal agreements related to children or assets

Insurance Policies:
Health insurance policies
Life insurance policies
Property and casualty insurance policies

Estate Planning Documents:
Wills
Trust documents
Powers of attorney
Health care directives

Communication Records:
Emails or text messages related to the divorce
Communications with your spouse or their attorney

Child-Related Documents:
Custody agreements or parenting plans
Records of child support payments or expenses
School records and schedules

Employment Information:
Employment contracts
Benefit information

Miscellaneous:
Social security numbers and birth certificates for all family members.

It's a good idea to consult with your attorney early in the process. Each situation will be different based on the presence of children, the financial situation, and state/local divorce laws. Consult with your legal counsel as early as possible.

#4. Your Hedge of Protection

Do you need to limit your communication with your ex? Now is not the time to try to *prove to yourself or others* that you can handle being in contact with your ex when you know it's an emotional or mental strain. If you want to prove something, prove that you are accountable for your well-being by taking action to protect yourself from unnecessary, emotionally debilitating situations. Your hedge of protection can include the following:

Limit direct communication. Use your legal representative. Use text or emails whenever possible. This will keep you from hearing their voice while also providing written documentation of your communication. Written documentation makes tracking timelines, reviewing requests, and establishing roles and responsibilities easier.

Social media block. Decrease the temptation by removing access. Block them on Facebook, Instagram, LinkedIn, etc. You will not have easy access to view their profiles and vice versa.

Remove Shared Location Apps and Devices. If you use devices like Apple Air Tags - disengage them. If you used the Share Location feature on your phone or other devices - stop sharing. If you have access to your ex through a tracking device, delete the connection from your end.

Write it down first. When direct communication is required, write down the key points you want to share. Stick to your list. Stay emotionally grounded by focusing on the list, not your ex's tone, tendencies, or attempts to annoy you.

Have an escape plan. When interactions are necessary, have someplace to go, something to do, or a reason for ending the conversation. Then, end it. Be calm, clear, and cordial.

Friendly versus Friends. You do not have to be friends with your ex. That is a complete sentence. It doesn't make you a mean person, weak, or a person failing at practicing their faith. When children are involved, there is good cause to establish a respectful and cordial relationship. Be responsibly cordial and respectful.

***Say My Name, Say My Name?* Not!** Create distance. Distance can be physical, emotional, mental, or otherwise. In this case, it's literally avoiding saying their name. Internationally renowned Breakup & Divorce Coach Sara Davison suggests using your ex's initials when you refer to them. For years, I created nicknames like lawyer man, dentist guy, and cross-dress man (a long and interesting story for another book). But these nicknames are so effective that I struggle to remember real names, and my friends and family only identify some of the people from my past by their nicknames.

#5. Have Fun

It might be the last thing on your mind these days. Fun. Laughter. Levity. Games. Your brain needs a break. You need a way to release tension. Doing something fun is a relief for your mind, body, and emotional self. Here are a few things you can do for fun that are low budget.

- Play jacks or whatever game you might've played growing up. Hopscotch, jump rope, and hula hoop come to mind. Don't judge me, but I have jacks and a hula hoop in my office right now.

- Date night with or without someone else: dinner and a movie, a picnic in the park, at the beach, or in your living room. Get creative. Do you have a good friend who lives out of town? Schedule a virtual date night. The two of you can each bring your favorite beverage and snacks, get in your cozy pajamas, and enjoy wonderful conversation. If you use Zoom, you can pull up a movie online and watch it together. Or plan a visit!

Spending time with a dear friend and enjoying the change of scenery could be just what the doctor ordered.

- Bowling, tennis, pickleball, or some activity you enjoy.

- Take a walk somewhere new. Be safety conscious.

- Pamper yourself. A hot bath, relaxing music, your favorite beverage, and a book or a movie at home.

- Have an orgasm. Yep, you read that right. An orgasm is an incredible way to tap into your sensual side while also releasing tension. But don't take my word for it. Researchers have concluded that orgasms cause a release of dopamine, a pleasure chemical. This release redirects your attention away from stress towards pleasure. Orgasms also release oxytocin, which calms your nervous system and leads to an increased production of the sleep hormone melatonin. Yep, an orgasm may be your ticket to a good night's sleep. There are many more benefits credited to orgasms, but I'll end with this one—body confidence! Yes, learning how to have an orgasm on your own can be empowering on many levels.

#6. Destination Clutter Cleanse™

Destination Clutter Cleanse™ (DCC) is a six-part, self-paced course that guides you through cleaning and creating a space that reflects who you are—today.

Breakups and divorces can leave people walking through rooms and using furniture and appliances that serve as constant reminders of an ex or situations they had with their ex that they want to forget. No matter how many people tell you, "It's just a sofa!", that sofa could be triggering for you. Whether the sofa is where you had the worst arguments, experienced some form of abuse, or it's where your partner proposed—the memories could be emotionally troublesome.

You are the only person who knows what that feels like, and you have the power to change it. Replacing a piece of furniture, repurposing it, or finding a creative way to cover it up can be both effective in helping you dial down your emotions and empowering!

The Destination Clutter Cleanse™ Program provides a step-by-step process that will move you through assessing and repurposing the space, purging, figuring out what stays, creating your space, and finally, celebrating.

Here are three steps from the Destination Clutter Cleanse™ process you can do now to make a difference in one room.

Deep clean. Whether you do it yourself or hire someone, a thorough cleaning always makes you feel better. Look for eco-friendly cleaning products so you aren't "cleaning" your space with toxic products. What to include:

- Dust everything from the ceilings down the walls.

- Clean the light fixtures.

- Remove everything from shelves, bookcases, tabletops.

- Wipe or polish the furniture.

- Wipe/wash the windowsills and baseboards.

- Clean the windows.

- Wash and polish the floors.

- Air out or replace bed pillows and throw pillows.

- Weather permitting, open the windows while you're cleaning.

- Bonus: Cleaning is also a pretty good workout.

Reposition furniture. Relocate your furniture. Move the bed to a different wall. Rotate the furniture in the living room. Changing the layout of a room can alter how you navigate in the space and that alone can change the feel of the room enough to help you dissociate the space from problematic thoughts and feelings.

Perhaps the cost of replacing an item prevents you from getting rid of it. In that case, I recommend you cover it. In one case, a client used a throw and decorative pillows to change the look of the sofa.

Paint. Still one of the least expensive ways to make the greatest impact in a room is to paint. Two gallons of paint will do most average size rooms and the difference can be grand and mood changing. Whether you do it yourself or hire someone, take a few steps to ensure you get the desired results:

1. Get a finish that is appropriate for the room. Example: You typically don't want flat paint in the bathroom.

2. Put color swatches on the walls and live with them for a few days before selecting a color.

3. If you do it yourself, watch videos and take the proper precautions to protect everything in the room that can't be moved out in advance.

4. Be sure you befriend someone in the paint department at your local store and ensure you have all the correct supplies.

5. If this is your first time painting, do one wall completely so you aren't overwhelmed by doing an entire room.

6. Take your time and do it right.

7. Have fun!

#7. Work on Wellness

For most people, the three things below are things you can start working on today.

The first thing – sleep well. There aren't enough pages in this book for me to tell you how important sleep is and how detrimental to your well-being it is if you're not getting enough quality sleep. There are two TED talks I recommend you watch as soon as possible. Both are by Matt Walker, Ph.D. They are, *6 Tips for Better Sleep*, and *Sleep is Your Superpower*.

At a time when you are under considerable stress and likely feeling mentally and emotionally drained, it is important that you manage the things that are manageable. Learning to sleep well is something you can manage.

The second thing is for you to be mindful of what you're eating. If you are already a healthy eater, maintain that aspect of your self-care. If you know you could do better, this is a great time to improve your mindfulness around what you put in your body. Start with something simple like cutting down or eliminating added sugars, sodas, and alcohol. Then, figure out two or three healthier options you can introduce or enhance in your current nutrition plan. Is it to eat more whole foods, go plant-based, have more balanced and portion-controlled meals, or drink more water? Whatever you decide, write these things down, embrace the expectation of a good outcome, combine that with joyful anticipation of engaging in the process, and then do the darn thing.

Third, incorporate movement throughout your day. There's a difference between working out and movement. If you already workout consistently, that's great. Be sure that you are moving throughout the day, not working out once a day for 90 minutes, feeling great about it, and then sitting for the next 8-12 hours. Take a few minutes each hour to stand, walk around or in place, and stretch. Whenever possible, do what you can outdoors so you benefit from the sunlight.

As will all things, it's a good idea to consult with your physician if you are already dealing with health issues. There are specialist available to help you with sleep, nutrition, and movement – if you feel these are things you cannot tackle on your own.

<u>Empowering Reflection</u>

Respond to the following:

Did you jump to this chapter because you are dealing with a breakup or divorce now?

Do you understand how professional support can help you thrive, not just survive your experience?

Are you still stuck on page 89 where I gave you permission to have a self-induced orgasm and you're trying to remember if you know what that even feels like?

CHAPTER 7

Rites of Passage

"For a lot of people, divorce is an incredibly healthy move to make in their life."

— ADAM SCOTT

"I'm a minister. As much as I want to tell her to leave him, I just can't."

The comment doesn't surprise me. L.T. grew up attending Pentecostal churches that hold traditional beliefs about marriage. Communities where Malachi 2:16 is interpreted as, "God hates divorce."

> Does the Bible say, "God hates divorce?" And if yours does, is your Bible wrong?

This conversation isn't about either of us changing the other's mind. We are brainstorming. Exploring potential options for a woman in a marriage that has all the signs of emotional abuse.

"Hey, I get it," I tell L.T. "Nobody wants to feel like they are promoting divorce. Nobody enters their marriage preparing for it to end. Divorce is not a destination. Divorce is a place where some of our relationships end, but it's not where we want to get stuck. Shouldn't we be able to count on our churches, pastors, and ministry leaders to support us in having the tools we need to navigate divorce when it happens?"

"You need to write that down!" L.T. says immediately.

"Write what down?"

"What you said, *Divorce Is Not A Destination*. Write *that* down."

At that moment, I communicate something that makes sense to me. Nobody gets married planning for divorce.

While I can understand that many ministers might feel obligated to do everything in their power to save a marriage, the responsibility should be to the individuals involved, not the institution. No one ministers to an institution. And to quote Kristian A. Smith, Founding Pastor of The Faith Community, "Doctrine is not the same as divinity."

How we come to believe what we believe about marriage and divorce is sometimes connected more to doctrine, which is part of our socialization rather than divinity. And in the United States, we condition children to think about marriage very early on.

My First Wedding Gift

"I heavy it. I heavy it."

At two, I've decided to pick up Nana's leaded crystal vase that, until now, was sitting in the center of her coffee table.

As I'm walking it to her, her eyes grow wider with each of my carefully placed, unstable steps. As I struggle with the weight of the vase, and the look of fear on her face, my two-year-old brain mashes, *I'm bringing it to you and it's heavy*, into *I heavy it. I heavy it.*

Unfortunately, my delivery attempt is thwarted. Just before I clear the coffee table, the weight becomes too much, and I lose my grip on the vase. It hits the edge of the marble tabletop breaking a piece from the base. Nana's face transforms from anxious to annoyed. Without missing a beat, she says,

"This is going to be your wedding present."

At the age of two, I inherit my first wedding gift.

There are no wedding artifacts around me growing up. None. In my grandparent's home, there isn't one wedding picture of the two of them or any other family members. There are no wedding pictures of my parents' wedding. Only two weddings exist in my childhood memories. My mother's marriage to Perry, and my aunt Janis and Uncle Dennis' wedding. I am nine or ten years old by the time their ceremonies happen.

Unless my memory fails me, I don't recall attending another wedding in my family until I got married for the first time about eighteen years later. True to her word, Nana gives me that leaded crystal vase with the broken base as a wedding present. But why is my wedding on her mind when I'm just two years old?

Weddings, Marriages, and Family

Let's face it, we love weddings. People who don't want to get married get excited when someone they care about is planning a wedding. Who doesn't beam at the site of a lavish venue or swoon over a couple's plan to exchange vows in a private tropical oasis? Family heirlooms are set aside, and although we may hate missing the ceremony, we still cheer for friends who return blushed and happily tethered after eloping.

It's evident that my imagination is largely influenced by a culture that places a high premium on the institution of marriage. Dreaming of getting married is a universal pastime for children and many adults. One could say weddings are one of our national pastimes.

Between 2001 and 2017, the United States government spent upwards of 1 billion dollars on the Healthy Marriage Initiative. After spending three years and 500 hours researching the program and interviewing 45 low-income parents who took classes within the program; author and researcher Jennifer M. Randles described the Healthy Marriage Initiative program as promoting:

"a pro-marriage culture in which two-parent married families are considered the healthiest. It also assumes that marriage can be a socioeconomic survival mechanism for low-income families, and an engine of upward mobility."

What Ms. Randles further noted is that any program or policy designed to promote family stability and equality must include what she refers to as, "the intimate inequalities that lead to curtailed commitments." Finally, she used the term "mind-boggling" to describe the pressure placed on marriage and government-funded programs to be the panacea that breaks poverty. Ms. Randle and I agree that we are a nation that seems to idolize weddings.

Weddings are a $70 billion dollar industry in the United States. **We idolize weddings to the tune of nearly 6,000 weddings per day** at an average cost between $28k to $35k per wedding.

One could argue that we spend significantly more time, money, and attention on weddings and honeymoons than we do preparing to be a supportive, loving person and partner. We focus on bridesmaid's dresses and venues instead of family dynamics. Today social media "likes" appears to be more important than mending familial relationships, bonding with future in-laws, and creating a support system that may prove beneficial when the honeymoon phase ends, or the relationship ends in divorce.

Pop Quiz

Check the boxes that are true for you:

God hates divorce.

The Bible says God hates divorce.

I learned divorce was bad from church.

I learned divorce was bad from my family.

I believe people who get divorced won't get into Heaven.

I feel bad about myself because of my divorce; or I would feel bad about myself if I were divorced.

People who get divorced should've tried harder.

Divorce was a gift I gave to myself, and I celebrated the experience.

Here is where I invite you to open your mind to ideas about marriage and divorce that may be vastly different from what you have been socialized to believe is acceptable or normal. Let's start with the *walking marriage*.

The Walking Marriage

The Mosuo intrigue me from the moment I learn about them as I'm watching the first episode of the series *Harlem*. In the show, Meghan Good's character plays an anthropology professor. She is telling her class about the Mosuo. When she begins talking about the *walking marriage*, I pause the show and Google Mosuo. For a moment, I don't believe what she is saying is real. It absolutely is!

The Mosuo live high in the Himalayas and are said to be one of the last semi-matriarchal societies in the world. Women are highly regarded for their motherhood. They also play a dominant and primary role in leadership, property rights, and social privilege.

The *walking marriage* is an ancient custom that favors female agency over male dependency. Women choose and change partners as they wish. There is no stigma, guilt, shame, or backlash associated with the practice of this cultural tradition. Children are reared with the woman's family, and uncles help raise the children by providing consistent male guidance. The male–female relationships are private, with men visiting their prospective female partners by going to her home at night after the woman has given him permission to do so.

What are your first thoughts about the Mosuo culture where marriage and divorce as we know it doesn't exist?

- Did you judge them based on your religious beliefs?

- Did you think, "Oh, my goodness this sounds like heaven?"

- Did you think, "These people are all going straight to hell!"

- Were you so curious you stopped reading to go learn more about them?

- Did you hear Tabitha Brown's voice in your head saying, "Mind your business"?

This *walking marriage* may seem odd to you. Just as the fact that we continue to fight for reproductive rights might seem odd to a Mosuo woman. Rather than judge, explore the fact that the Mosuo developed a system based on love and mutual affection where each person is afforded an equitable measure of freedom.

A Mauritanian Divorce Celebration

As the Mosuo live without the formality of marriage, thereby eliminating the need for divorce, the women of Mauritania live in a community that celebrates divorce. For a Mauritanian woman, divorce represents the return to a place of dignity and repose. Her mother and sisters welcome her back to the family's home. She is honored at parties and dinners amidst the sounds of tambourines and the celebratory trills of Zaghrouta, a long, wavering, high-pitched cry. Ironically, these are the same celebratory sounds you would hear at a Mauritanian wedding.

Friends organize lavish events with music and poetry. Attendees hire poets to praise their newly divorced friend for her beauty and virtues. Poetry is a key aspect of Mauritanian society. And because divorced women are known to evoke the passions of poets, it is common for a divorce celebration to include poetry that praises the honoree while reminding her of the eligible men who will line up to ask for her hand now that she is once again single.

In some parts of Mauritania, the divorce party is organized by a bachelor. This celebration is called a Tahrish, and it is done to make her husband jealous in hopes that he will reconsider his decision to divorce. At the Tahrish, the bachelor showers the divorced woman with praise, while admonishing the husband for being so foolish as to let such a "rare rose" leave his home.

In Mauritania, multiple marriages signify a woman's uniqueness, beauty, and attractiveness. Men view divorced women as more experienced, which makes them more desirable than single women.

The Woman at the Well

The third story is from John Chapter 4 of the Bible when Jesus encounters a Samaritan woman at a well. The often-noted aspects of this meeting include the fact that men and women did not engage socially unless they were related. Also, Jews reportedly hated Samaritans and went out of their way to avoid interacting with them. More harsh commentary brands the woman at the well as promiscuous, a prostitute, and a sinner.

Nevertheless, Jesus engages her in conversation.

"13 Jesus answered and said to her, "Whoever drinks of this water will thirst again, 14 but whoever drinks of the water that I shall give him will never thirst. But the water that I shall give him will become in him a fountain of water springing up into everlasting life.""

15 The woman said to Him, "Sir, give me this water, that I may not thirst, nor come here to draw."

16 Jesus said to her, **"Go, call your husband,** and come here.""

17 The woman answered and said, **"I have no husband."**

Jesus said to her, **"You have well said, 'I have no husband,'** 18 for you have had five husbands, and the one whom you now have is not your husband; in that **you spoke truly."** - John 13-18, NKJV

28 The woman then left her waterpot, **went her way into the city, and said to the men,** 29 "Come, see a Man who told me all things that I ever did. Could this be the Christ?" 30 Then they went out of the city and came to Him. - John 28-30, NKJV

And many of the Samaritans of that city **believed in Him because of the word of the woman** who testified, **"He told me all that I ever did."** - John 39, NKJV

There are three aspects of her story I want you to consider. First, how she spoke the truth about having had five husbands and currently being with a man who was not her husband. Understand that the Samaritan woman lived during a time when girls were married off by their fathers. Some as young as thirteen. And while five husbands may have been unusual, it was common for a woman to remarry after being widowed or divorced.

In her book *The Samaritan Woman's Story: Reconsidering John 4 After #ChurchToo*, Caryn A. Reeder sees that Jesus did not command this woman to repent. Calling to question the unflattering accusations of some scholars. We don't know the details of her circumstances, and I contend that they weren't relevant to her purpose.

Second, women had little social capital. Yet, Jesus revealed himself to her, making her the unlikely messenger of his arrival.

Third, her word led many to believe in Him. Reeder interpreted this as a sign that the Samaritan woman garnered a level of respect amongst some members of the community. They believed in Jesus because of this woman's testimony. Others needed to see for themselves, but many believed based on her word alone.

Customs, Traditions, and Mores

What we have in common with the Mosuo, the women of Mauritania and the Samaritan woman at the well, is that we are also influenced and sometimes challenged by customs, traditions, and social norms. It is easier to criticize and discredit than it is to appreciate and respect differences. When something doesn't align with what we believe, we label it wrong.

What a wonderful world it would be if we could live on this Earth together without feeling compelled to create right and wrong or good and bad from differences that cause no harm.

You may not embrace the Mosuo's *walking marriage,* but learning about them might give you the courage to walk away from a toxic relationship. If you're a single parent, struggling to do it all alone, perhaps the Mosuo's tradition will lead you to intentionally create a support circle for yourself and your child. Consider including your ex so there is a strong co-parenting component built in.

Have you been embarrassed by the prospect of getting a divorce? Use the women of Mauritania as models of what transitioning through divorce can be like. This doesn't mean ignoring or denying the emotional roller coaster you will likely experience as you navigate the

Loss Cycle. This means you can also create a ceremony that embraces the transition rather than being embarrassed by it.

Ironically, divorce parties, with themed cakes and all, are on the rise here in the United States. So, maybe we are catching on.

Finally, you can be encouraged by The Woman at the Well. She was neither defined nor deterred because of her marital status. She stepped into her purpose. Wouldn't you prefer to step into the next phase of life with grace, ease, and the empowering message of *you are more than enough?*

Whether your perspective on divorce is based on faith-supported doctrine, cultural traditions, familial pressures, or some

Fun Fact

The Bible, and therefore many Bible readers, continue to hold to a misinterpretation of Malachi 2:16. As I researched for *Divorce Is Not a Destination*, I realized that several of my Bibles contain the old misinterpretation. If your Bible reads: "God hates divorce," or "I hate divorce," and "I" is referring to God, it may be time for you to get a new version of the Bible as well.

From 1611 to approximately 1996, most major Bibles interpreted Malachi 2:16 as shown above. The verse was viewed as being anti-divorce. However, for hundreds of years before 1611, and after the publishing of the Dead Sea Scrolls in 1996, the text was viewed as an anti-treachery verse and interpreted as such:

"The man who hates and divorces his wife," says the Lord, the God of Israel, "does violence to the one he should protect, "says the Lord Almighty." Mal 2:16 NIV

Visit:
www.lifesavingdivorce.com/malachi

combination of the above, ask yourself *how is what you believe serving you;*

or how well are you able to serve holding onto your current belief? Challenge any belief that causes you to feel inadequate, insecure, or insignificant. You have the power to decide what is best for you. Your destiny is counting on you to do so.

Empowering Reflection

1. Do you want to love yourself into being the best version of who God designed you to be?

2. Have you been a source of negativity to yourself because of how you view and internalize being divorced?

3. If you answered "yes" to #2, what does it feel like for you to acknowledge that?

Write for 10 minutes about what you believe you need to change so you are leading your best self forward and serving at your highest level.

CHAPTER 8

A Personal – Personnel Problem

"You don't have to leave your heart at home when you go to work."

— ANONYMOUS

"I operated at about 10% after my divorce. I did enough to keep my job."

This is what book coach and best-selling author Teresa de Grosbois shares about trying to function at work after her divorce.

"There was no support. I just worked in a fog."

Working Through Divorce

Corporate wellness programs offer support for everything from tobacco cessation and stress management to mental health support, fitness trackers, and gym memberships. When wellness programs include parental and family support, people like Teresa are still likely to feel unsupported. Why? Because rarely, if ever, do these programs mention or provide specific assistance for people going through divorce. The stakes are even higher and resources just as lacking when domestic violence is involved. Corporate policies that address breakups, divorces, and domestic violence are vital.

The Good: Escape and Renew

The Holmes-Rahe Stress Inventory rates divorce just below the stress associated with the death of a spouse, highlighting the significant challenges divorce poses. However, each divorce experience is unique. The "Life Events and Work Study" from the University of Minnesota sheds light on this, affirming what many of us know first-hand. It ain't always all bad. Nearly 39% of the participants reported a positive impact on their job, work, and career because of their divorce.[7] Two primary reasons surfaced that speak to why some people navigate divorce and emerge with a newfound strength and determination in their careers.

For some, the workplace is a sanctuary—an escape from the tumultuous emotions and challenges associated with divorce. Being immersed in work is a diversion, that allows them to temporarily distance themselves from the stress of their personal lives. The act of focusing on professional responsibilities becomes a cathartic exercise, because they can channel their energy and attention into tasks that contribute positively to their career.

In cases where participants labeled their relationships as dysfunctional, they found they had more time and mental bandwidth to dedicate to their jobs. The absence of the stressors inherent in a troubled marriage allowed for increased focus, creativity, and productivity at work.

The second reason divorce yielded positive outcomes at work for some participants was that divorce became a catalyst for self-reflection and personal growth, which led to a renewed sense of purpose concerning their careers.

This renewed motivation translates into a proactive approach to career development. These participants set their sights on being more than just employees; they were determined to be exceptional contributors in

---

[7] (Wanberg, Csillag and Duffy 2023)

their respective workplaces. The experience of navigating the complexities of divorce instills resilience, determination, and a heightened awareness of the importance of self-improvement. These individuals strive for upward mobility, seeing their careers as avenues for personal redemption and fulfillment.

The Bad: Negative Affect and Distracted

It's encouraging to know that some emerge from divorce with newfound strength in their professional lives. But there is a flip side. In the same University of Minneapolis study, 44% of the participants reported that divorce caused problems in the workplace. Researchers Wanberg, Csillag, and Duffy highlighted two major themes illuminating divorce's negative impact on employees' work experiences.

One theme participants identified could be described as a brewing internal storm that affected the daily professional landscape. The researchers referred to it as an "intrusive negative affect at work."[8]

It manifested in employees being moody, depressed, irritable, disengaged, and even short-tempered. The emotional toll of divorce can lead to periods of despondency and melancholy, making it challenging to maintain a consistent and positive presence in the workplace. The struggle to navigate through the emotional turbulence can impact work relationships, productivity, and overall job satisfaction.

The second negative theme that emerged from the study is characterized by "reduced focus and rumination at work."[9] Divorce can be a distractor, making it difficult for individuals to concentrate on their professional responsibilities. This reduced focus is not just a fleeting distraction but a persistent challenge that affects day-to-day work life.

---

[8] (Wanberg, Csillag and Duffy 2023)
[9] (Wanberg, Csillag and Duffy 2023)

Employees grappling with the aftermath of divorce may find themselves mentally preoccupied with the issues surrounding childcare, finances, real estate, and more. The constant rumination on the past, present, and future aspects of the divorce process can create a mental fog, hindering their ability to engage fully in their work tasks.

The Ugly: Domestic Violence

Earning a master practitioner accreditation to work with individuals after a breakup or divorce involved a second tier of study, with The Dash Charities, a UK regulated domestic abuse center. The additional training equips practitioners with the tools needed to support individuals who were in toxic or difficult relationships. Toxic could be anything from experiencing power and control dynamics to recovering from one or more types of domestic violence.

Before I connect this to the workplace, here are statistics you may find startling. Reportedly 23.5% of divorces are caused by domestic violence. Seventy-two percent of murder-suicides involve an intimate partner, and 94% of those victims are women. During their lifetime, 1 in 4 women in the United States will be abused by an intimate partner. Among working adult men and women, that number is 1 in 5.

Finally, the leading cause of death for women at work is homicide. More must be done to support employees dealing with breakups, divorces, and domestic violence.

A Personal-Personnel Problem

According to the Center for Disease Control and Prevention (CDC) businesses pay $729 million per year in lost productivity related to domestic violence. Domestic violence, domestic abuse, intimate partner violence—no matter what you call it, it's time we all realize that it's not a private matter.

According to Life Innovations, Inc., Relationship-related stress costs

US businesses upwards of $300 billion annually. On average, employees lose 168 hours of work annually after their divorce.[10] The Grief Recovery Institute reported that divorce-related stress is responsible for nearly $75 billion dollars in pay or productivity losses. Given this information, it's easy to understand how the adverse impact of divorce is not limited to the person going through the breakup. While the employee going through a divorce can experience a 40% decrease in productivity for up to 3 years, they are not alone. Both co-workers and supervisors are likely to experience decreases in productivity as well.

It's been reported that nearly 70% of employees may be dealing with the effects of divorce at any given time. Unfortunately, colleagues and supervisors are often unaware that divorce is the cause of the uncharacteristic lack of concentration and decrease in engagement their colleague is experiencing. The reason they are unaware might be related to the researchers who found that 92% of employees confess that they would not say anything to HR if they were going through a divorce, and 95% would not share with HR that they were going through a breakup. Hence, it's quite possible they are also reluctant to share that information with coworkers.

Here are three reasons I believe someone at work would be reluctant to share that they are going through a breakup or divorce. First, a lack of psychological safety. Again, I remind you that I'm not a therapist or psychologist. Feel free to check with one to delve deeper. A person is less likely to take an interpersonal risk if they perceive the consequences will result in being ridiculed, punished, or marginalized.

The second reason has to do with the organizational culture and the leadership. What is the tone that's been set by leadership and the prevailing culture? Do employees generally feel comfortable having conversations about personal aspects of their lives, or is this taboo?

---

[10] (Turvey, 2017)

Do leaders model behavior by sharing aspects of life outside of work? If people aren't comfortable bringing up non-work-related issues, they will unlikely be comfortable sharing something as personal as divorce.

The third reason people may be reluctant to share is past experiences. Whether they experienced it or witnessed it, seeing how sharing information was handled or mishandled previously could determine whether a person is willing to divulge such personal information now.

Individuals and leaders can consider the 5Ps:

Policies – are a set of guidelines or rules, often written in an employee handbook.

Principles – are foundational beliefs or values, often the guiding force behind decision-making and behavior.

Practices – are the methods or behaviors that align with the principles and policies—policies and principles in action.

Procedures – detail the specific steps or methods for tasks.

Programs – are organized initiatives with specific objectives.

The 5Ps provide an employee with a tangible way to assess psychological safety and gauge the potential receptiveness of culture and leadership to the needs of someone going through a breakup or divorce. This isn't a foolproof method because organizations often espouse values that they do not practice. Still, the absence of several or all the 5Ps might sound an alarm to proceed with caution.

The current national statistics are unfavorable. Fewer than 18% of US organizations offer specific programs that support employees through their breakup or divorce process. No surprise that more than 90% of employees elect not to share their breakup or divorce status with HR.

Your employer offers specific breakup and divorce coaching.

> Yes
>
> No
>
> I have no idea.

You or a coworker have struggled with productivity because of a breakup or divorce.

> Yes
>
> No
>
> I don't speak with my coworkers.

You would or would've taken advantage of a breakup/divorce coach if it were available through your company's wellness program.

> Yes
>
> No
>
> Nobody needs this kind of help. People need to keep their personal lives at home.
>
> Your part of the 92-95% that would never tell your employer you were going through a breakup or divorce.

The 5Ps in Action

Making it personal requires that employers acknowledge the inevitable fact that challenges experienced in one's personal life are likely to manifest as challenges at work. Leaders must be invested in cultivating a culture of compassion. Support for individuals navigating a breakup or divorce must be infused into several, if not all, the 5Ps, and cultivated within the corporate culture.

Here's an example of how a company might use policies, principles, practices, procedures, and a program to support individuals going through a divorce:

Policies

Divorce Support Policy: The company establishes a policy that recognizes the emotional and practical challenges faced by employees going through a divorce. This policy emphasizes the organization's commitment to supporting affected employees without discrimination or stigma.

Principles

Compassionate Support: The company's guiding principle is to offer compassionate support, respect employees' privacy, and ensure fairness and equity in all interactions concerning divorce-related issues.

Practices

Confidential Counseling: The company offers confidential counseling services through its Employee Assistance Program (EAP) to help employees navigate emotional and psychological challenges, including breakups and divorces.

Flexible Work Arrangements: Recognizing the need for flexibility during such times, the company allows affected employees to adjust their work schedules, work remotely if feasible, or take intermittent leave.

Resource Referral: HR provides employees with a list of external resources, such as legal advisors specializing in family law, financial counselors, and support groups.

Procedures

Reporting and Communication: The company establishes a clear procedure for employees to inform HR or their managers about their situation if they wish to seek support or adjustments. This process ensures confidentiality and sensitivity.

Accommodation Requests: Detailed procedures outline how employees can request specific accommodations, such as temporary changes in workload or responsibilities, requesting time off for court or attorney appointments, and managing school and childcare that has changed because of the breakup. This could also include the process for evaluating and implementing these requests.

Documentation: Procedures specify the types of documentation required (e.g., a letter from a legal advisor or counselor) to support accommodation requests and the confidentiality measures for handling such documentation.

Program

Divorce Support Program: The company launches or provides access to a comprehensive program aimed at providing holistic support to employees navigating divorce. This program might include:

- **Professional Strategy Sessions:** Group learning and development sessions; or individual strategic coaching sessions conducted by a breakup and divorce practitioner.

- **Workshops and Seminars**: Regular workshops on topics like managing stress, financial planning post-divorce, and co-parenting strategies.

- **Peer Support Groups**: Facilitated support groups where employees can share experiences, seek advice, and receive emotional support from colleagues who have gone through similar experiences.

- **Legal and Financial Consultations**: Partnerships with legal and financial experts to provide free or subsidized consultations to employees.

- **Wellness Resources**: Access to wellness resources, such as meditation sessions, yoga classes, or resilience-building workshops, to help employees cope with emotional and mental health challenges.

Some organizations in the UK have successfully implemented initiatives that support employees going through a divorce by essentially treating the HR policies as they would handle bereavement leave. Companies like Asda, Metro Bank, Tesco, Unilever, and PwC are among the organizations promoting what's been deemed more family-friendly workplace policies related to separation and divorce.

By integrating policies, principles, practices, procedures, and dedicated programs, companies can create supportive environments that acknowledge the personal challenges of divorce and provide practical resources and accommodations to help affected employees navigate this difficult period.

<u>Empowering Reflections</u>

1. If you've gone through a breakup or divorce that impacted your job performance, spend 5-10 minutes writing about your experience.

2. Find out if your company offers specific breakup and divorce coaching by accredited professionals.

3. If your company had the 5Ps, Policies, Principles, Practices, Procedures, and Programs that clearly supported individuals navigating a difficult breakup or divorce, how might it have changed your experience at work?

Divorce Is Not A Destination®

CHAPTER 9

Create a Vision Network

*"Holding on is believing that there's only a past; letting
go is knowing that there's a future."*

— DAPHNE ROSE KINGMA

"I'm going to buy this house."

It's winter in Illinois. My business partner Rodney and I have just walked into a townhome. We're standing on the protective adhesive plastic that stretches over the living room carpet. Good thing. It's winter and there is snow melting from our boots.

We haven't made it through the living room, and already, I know this will be my home. There's no way to explain how I know. I just do.

Rodney and his wife Charlene are purchasing a home down the street. He has been telling me about two empty townhouses at the end of the dead-end street. Today is the day I decide to see their future home and walk through the empty townhomes down the block.

The property sits next to the golf course driving range and across the street from the clubhouse. The original contractor sold the development and it's been unoccupied for twelve years and counting.

Before we've stepped off the carpet onto the hardwood flooring into the kitchen, I am certain I will be the first owner of this house.

<u>Pop Quiz</u>

How do you address pursuing a gigantic dream?

- Scare yourself out of going for it because you might fail.

- Quit as soon as it gets difficult.

- Go for something easier even if you don't want it, so you feel accomplished.

- Don't dream and then you don't have to bother with any of this.

On paper, I have no business thinking about purchasing this townhome. The condo I currently live in needs to sell before I can buy the house I want, and I don't have it listed yet. Then there's the fact that I was fired a few months ago. Granted, it was one of the most toxic work environments I'd ever worked in; nevertheless, it was generating income. Fortunately, unemployment is making it possible for me to do consulting work. Then there's my credit score and my savings, neither are where they need to be for me to apply for a mortgage.

Periodically, I drive the 45 minutes to the property and walk through what I've started referring to as *my e*mpty unit. There's always a reason to stop by Rodney and Charlene's place. When I do, it's inevitable. At some point, I say,

"Let's go down the street and look at my place!"

Rodney accommodates me. He knows the routine well enough that sometimes, he asks the obvious,

"Do you want to drive down and walk through *your* place?"

Once inside, I go through my routine. It starts with taking pictures and video. Next, I imagine where the furniture will go, what colors I will paint the rooms, and how I will redesign the kitchen cabinets. Rodney waits, fully aware that the visit isn't complete until he hears me say,

"Wait, I have to run down and see the basement!"

Off I go. Excited, like it's the first time I've bolted down these stairs.

When time allows, we walk across the street, through the parking lot, to the golf course café. They have the best hot dogs. The staff is beginning to recognize me and ask questions like,

"Have you moved in yet?!"

"No, not yet" is always my response.

Nothing deters me or dampens my spirits regarding my belief that I will own this townhome. I accept the property manager, Eddie's invitation to attend an open house. He has arranged for realtors, brokers, and investors to see the two remaining units, hoping to attract a buyer. While there, I introduce myself and let everyone know the attached unit is available. This one is mine.

The typical response is, "Congratulations. When do you close on *this* unit?"

"I'm not under contract yet. The unit is waiting for me to buy it." I smile, leaving confused and amused looks in my wake.

I remain undeterred. Even on the day that Eddie tells me, "I found buyers. The unit is under contract to a couple."

"Eddie, if that's God's will, I will purchase the attached unit." I continue, "I hope the people won't be too disappointed when it doesn't go through because until God tells me otherwise, that is my house."

Eddie is shaking his head. The look on his face reads, *She isn't getting it. These people are about to buy this unit.*

The 10th-floor condo I'm living in becomes the second home I list for sale without a realtor. I create the sales video, take all the pictures, and list it with a do-it-yourself service called *For Sale by Owner.* If you are considering handling your home sale without a realtor, I recommend you do your homework and consult with several realtors and a real estate attorney before deciding what works best for you.

Equipped with a Bluetooth remote access lock system, I can give access to my condo while traveling. It takes about three months for the right buyers to find it and a few more weeks to finalize the agreement.

Homeless and Hope-filled

"I love it! I'll buy it. It is going to be perfect in my new house!"

I've driven 45 minutes to meet a guy about some flooring. I'm standing in the backyard of a property looking at 1200 sq. ft. of African Walnut flooring. It is gorgeous.

The owner is selling it because there isn't enough flooring for the house he just purchased. I've looked at the ad on Facebook Marketplace every day since I found it two weeks ago while visiting my mom in California.

Now, I'm back in Illinois staring at it, and I know—this is my flooring.

He says, "I'm happy to sell this to you. I can see how much you appreciate the quality of the wood. When can I deliver it?"

"Oh. Well, I don't own the house yet."

He smiles, "No problem. We can get a date set for after closing."

I realize this may sound a little shady, but I'm putting all my cards on the table,

"So, I don't have a closing date either. I'm not under contract yet."

At this point, I will understand if he says he will keep looking for a buyer. All I can conclude is that my honesty about my situation and the sheer sincerity in my desire to own this flooring eventually wins him over. He agrees to sell it, hold it for me, and deliver it to me—once I own something with floors.

In the meantime, my vision network is taking shape. My dear friend Dr. Gail is supportive and practical. She asks me about the townhouse and then follows up with,

"Are you looking for other houses? Just in case this one doesn't come through."

I know she's forgotten that my backup plan is the adjoining townhouse. Just the same, I spend some time checking for other listings in the area.

Ultimately, my home sat for two years from the day I first saw it. I am convinced it waited for me. It waited through Eddie's open house, two contracts with other buyers, me selling my condo, and several issues with the Appraiser. I even had a mishap where the IRS deducted $6700 from my savings account for taxes I had already paid.

It is days before closing, and I'm short of what I need. Fortunately, my Sister April jumped in and loaned me money until the IRS could mail me my refund.

Two weeks after closing and a couple of months after finding the flooring, three young men from the church arrive to help unload my African Walnut flooring. The seller pulls up with the load on his flatbed. His girlfriend is with him.

He says, "We both wanted to see a house that sat for two years waiting for you to buy it."

I smile, welcome them inside, and give the first tour of my new home.

Have a Vision

If you have nothing to believe in or nothing to desire, you don't need a network—you need a vision. What are the things you want for yourself? What do you desire? Do you believe you deserve the things that come to mind? What is your level of expectation? Are you living in anticipation or anxiety and frustration?

You must be the first full-fledged member of your vision network. Create the vision! Is it for a place to live or a travel destination? Is it for a partner or a travel companion? Do you desire a career or to own a business?

Create a Vision Network

Perhaps your vision network selection process will happen organically as mine did. I set out to create my vision network with two friends. Introducing them was my way for us to create this supportive, heart-centered accountability triad. My vision network provides fertile ground for me to plant the **A.A.C.T. In Joy**! seed.

Trusting myself made bringing my vision network members together a joy. They embrace and embody a vision network mentality. They show up with a spirit of giving and support. We don't always agree, but we are always in agreement that the most important thing is to give each person space to be fully themselves.

We don't try to change each other to make ourselves feel better. It's not ego-driven; its engagement driven. We may challenge each other and check one another, but we are always focused on our engagement levels.

In the *Divorce Is Not A Destination* Program, I invite clients to assemble their own vision network. A vision network combines your vision with a support team. Think of it as a few people who support you as you are curating your joy-filled journey. Imagine having a group of people who want for you what you want for yourself, even if they cannot see it with the same clarity that you do.

Some of the members of your vision network will be able to *see* or *sense* your dream. Others might not *see the vision* as you do, but they believe in your desire to pursue it and your ability to live into your vision. You will have your own versions of Rodney's, Kath's, and Dr. Gail's. You will also have some people who may not be ready to be part of your vision network.

It would have been easy for them to bombard me with the harsh reality by asking questions like, "How and why do you think a beautiful property, sitting near a golf course, will sit there indefinitely waiting for you to purchase it?" Why did I even think that made sense? Shouldn't I sell my place before getting my hopes up? "You're setting yourself up to be disappointed when that house sells to someone else." I did get those questions and comments, but not from my vision network.

The beautiful thing about a vision network is they know the vision is yours. It's yours to curate and embody. It's yours to believe in. Your network is there to support and believe in you.

Who to Consider - Who to Avoid

Personally, I think a smaller vision network is best. It shouldn't get to the point where someone must manage the group. You will realize that once you are firmly onboard with what is important to you, how few people you need to support you.

Everyone shouldn't be in your vision network, and you need to be ok with that. I could give you a list of people to avoid inviting into your vision network. Toxic, negative, controlling, and selfish are some of the traits or behaviors you'd be best to avoid. But at this point in the process, I'm going to say this: What feels right to you? Who feels like a person you can go to when you want to share dreams of your future and brainstorm ways of being a better you? Who is someone who will support you as you embrace making changes in your life? When you think of a particular person, is there hesitation or relief?

You have the answers inside of you. It's time to give yourself permission to listen to yourself.

Finally, there's one more thing about a Vision Network: It's for you, but it's not all about you. You become a Vision Network member there to support, encourage, and uplift the other team members as well. This is a 100% reciprocal relationship model.

Empowering Reflection

Can you think of two people who could make up your Vision Network?

1. _____

Why would this person make a good Vision Network Members?

2. _____

Why would this person make a good Vision Network
Members?

Why would they make a good Vision Network Member?
Then, answer this question for yourself?

What makes you a good Vision Network Member?

CHAPTER 10

In A.A.C.T.ion

"There is no sense in punishing your future for the mistakes of your past. Forgive yourself, grow from it, and then let it go."

— MELANIE KOULOURIS

"Good morning. We're here to cut down those three tall palm trees in your front yard."

The electric company contractor turns and points to three tall palm trees that line our front yard.

"They're growing too close to the electrical wires."

The trees are aligned just behind our massive, well-sculpted hedge. A majestic Bismarck palm sits in the center of the tall palms, creating a picture-perfect view from our front door.

The crew sits in two large trucks waiting. The truck with the cherry picker is parked directly in front of our property. Poised to hoist one of the men up to begin work.

My first thought is, *Oh no! They are not cutting down our palm trees!*

It's funny how many memories can flood your mind in an instant. In a flash, I am back at Nana and Gampy's, the big house on Fire Road. A place with no sidewalks or streetlights.

I laugh and relax.

The technician watches me raise my mug and sip my coffee. Unprepared for the smile I give him, his eyes widen. I notice a sigh, likely the relief in knowing I'm not going to make his job difficult today. No longer bracing for a fight, he returns the smile. And says,

"Thank you."

"Thank you!" I respond. It takes me a second to get perspective. I think to myself, *I live on a property where I can have three palm trees cut down.*

He raises his head slightly and smiles. Motioning to the crew to get started, he turns and heads to work. I close the door and turn into the living room.

With my back to the door, I take a moment to admire the incredible home my mother and I have created here in Southern California. Contentment and thankfulness wash over me.

A relationship that began four years ago brought me to this place we call home. Two things strike me as ironic. One is how, this time, it's my relationship story that has impacted my mother's living situation; and two, I am standing in the same spot I was standing when the door closed behind him after he left more than two years ago.

My mother jokes that I was picking paint colors to convert his workspace to my office before his U-Haul hit Main Street, less than three blocks away. It wasn't quite that quick or as easy emotionally as she makes it sound. But I appreciate her way of acknowledging my resolve and resilience.

Like most breakups and divorces, the pain and discomfort started before the end. The growing pains remind me of the angst you experience before you finally admit you have outgrown a favorite outfit. To salvage it, you let seams out. You move buttons over. After a few uncomfortable events where you squeeze yourself into a one-size-too-small body slimmer, you reach the point where you accept the *what is* of it all. It's time to let it go. It doesn't fit.

Unlike that favorite outfit, there's no passing the relationship off to a family member, friend, or a local thrift shop where you hope someone finds it who will appreciate the great condition it's in and wear it comfortably.

Instead, my ill-fitted experience leaves me with answers that have me wondering if I should've been asking myself different questions!

Even with a Master Practitioner Accreditation as a breakup and divorce coach, it can be a challenge to heed the advice I give others, 100% of the time. No one is immune to the emotions that a breakup or divorce can take you through. What I've learned and lived to prove is that there are tools and processes that will get me through the experience. And if I don't use them, I can spiral away from emotional stability like anyone else.

Writing *Divorce is Not a Destination* allowed me to examine how I put Accountability, Alignment, Communication, and Trust into A.A.C.T.ion for myself.

Accountability

Sometimes, I wonder if our relationship fell victim to the COVID-induced lockdown, which is credited with creating a perfect storm that fueled spikes in breakups and divorces around the world. However, even if that is the case, it's equally likely that the quarantine only unmasked pre-existing problems.

Fortunately, the pandemic led me to start weekly support calls with two dear friends. It is a bonus that they are also coaches. My mother is supportive, and my sisters provide both a sounding board when the anger kicks in and well-placed humor to help me *laugh to keep from crying*. There are plenty of crying episodes I could share with you.

Being a coach doesn't make me immune to experiencing the Loss Cycle (see Chapter 2). It's just that my life experiences and training position me to recover with a different awareness. But believe me when I tell you, wherever you are, I've probably been there.

Before I continue, I want to share a short list of activities that helped me take accountability this go 'round:

- Joining a gym
- Reading more than a dozen books in two months
- Journaling
- Dating myself with movie outings and trips to the Safari Park
- Being intentional about getting enough sleep and eating healthy meals
- Meditating and staying spiritually fed
- Removing the rose-colored glasses
- Avoiding negative people
- Blocking my ex on social media

Now, where was I?

One day it occurs to me that I am spending an incredible amount of time thinking about and talking about my ex. It's my mind analyzing and trying to answer questions about why he did what he did the way he did.

The questions that surface are things like: *What was he thinking?* And *How could he do this to me, to us!?* If these questions sound familiar, it's because they are often the questions, we ask ourselves when we want closure.

These questions torment me. Then I realize that I am tormenting myself with these questions. Let me repeat that so you can process it.

I am tormenting myself with these questions.

How so? Because they aren't questions that I can answer. They aren't my questions. Yes, I want closure, and I do all the typical things one does when attempting to get closure. I make calls that aren't answered or returned. When contact is finally made, I leave the call wondering,

How can he be angry with me?

What I realize is that I'm still asking myself questions that only he can answer. If I continue down this path, I only have myself to blame for how I'm feeling. That means it will be my fault, not his, if I choose to feel a certain way about how he's behaving. My unrealistic expectations of him do not make my emotions his responsibility.

Closure is relative. We set ourselves up for disappointment when we expect to get something from someone who doesn't have it to give or chooses not to give. It doesn't matter if they didn't meet your needs because they weren't cognizant, concerned, or capable. Whatever the reason, do you think it's realistic that you will get closure from this person? It's like going to an empty well for water.

This is what I offer to you now: Design closure for yourself.

I cannot control whether my ex takes my calls or how the conversation goes when we do speak. At first, this is frustrating. Then, I flip the script and decide that it's also empowering. Empowering because in this moment I become intentional about the things I read, what I listen to, and how I behave.

Two resources become tremendously helpful to me during this time. Byron Katie's book, *Loving What Is*, and *What to Say When You Talk to Yourself*, by Shad Helmstetter, Ph.D. In *Loving What Is*, Byron Katie challenges me to examine my role in my own life.

More importantly, I explore embracing what happened rather than spending a lot of time in denial or questioning why it happened. Dr.

Helmstetter's book helps me examine how I communicate to

Identify Your Inner Toxin

This is vital to rebuilding your confidence. You must identify what it is you say and think to yourself that is overriding your ability to live with confidence. That underlying belief will undermine you embracing and embodying a confident you. Once you identify it you must over-write the programming with positive beliefs you grow to embody.

myself throughout this experience. His book prompts me to ask the question: have negatively impactful thoughts been living in my head like old cobwebs? I also download Helmstetter's app "Self-Talk" and listen to it when I'm getting dressed in the morning. I don't judge it. I don't think about it. I listen.

For me, removing the rose-colored glasses meant acknowledging and writing down aspects of the relationship that were not going well—things my ex did that disturbed me, peaceful days or events that turned toxic, and hurtful words or actions. These are all elements we often ignore or deny in the belief that doing so supports a healthy relationship. However, in reality, we are only maintaining the *appearance* of a healthy relationship.

By writing down the problems and pain points, you remove the proverbial rose-colored glasses. Trust that you are strong enough to see things as they were and are. The good, the bad, the ugly.

Next, I decide to schedule a final session with Dave, the couples' therapist my ex and I had been seeing. Whether he knows it or not, this makes Dave part of my support team.

Near the end of my session, Dave recommends another book, *Attached* by Dr. Amir Levine and Rachel S. F. Heller. M.A. *Attached* describes different attachment styles that impact how we navigate relationships. The book includes an assessment that identifies your attachment style and that of your current or ex-partner. Since then, I have made this part of my DINAD Program because I think it's an incredible resource for people dealing with relationship issues. I also recommend a free attachment style assessment that's available online at: www.attachmenetproject.com. The Attachment Project site also offers tools for purchase to assist you in working through issues often associated with your specific attachment style.

Before I leave the session, Dave tells me the only way my relationship with my ex could have worked is if I had been willing to live with someone who is emotionally detached.

My response is, "That's not the kind of relationship I want to be in."

Dave's response is the most profound thing he has said during my time working with him.

"And that is a value-based decision you have the right to make for yourself."

Alignment

While I'm still months away from putting all the stages of the Loss Cycle behind me (see Chapter 2), Dave's response catapults me into deeper awareness and healing. *I have the right to make value-based decisions for myself.* Take a moment and say it out loud for yourself:

**I have the right to make value-based
decisions for myself.**

Remember, being in Alignment is about creating compatibility between your actions and what you value. Does how you show up reflect what's important to you?

In Chapter 7, I shared ways in which people from different cultures view and celebrate divorce. The Empowering Reflection from that chapter invites you to examine what you believe and how you feel about what you choose to believe regarding divorce.

How do you feel about challenging your beliefs? Are your beliefs based on your experiences and personal research? If your beliefs are associated with your faith, I invite you to read *Breaking All the Rules: An Ancient Framework for Modern Faith* by Kristian A. Smith. Pastor Smith masterfully encourages us to challenge belief systems that exist merely because they have existed. This includes your beliefs about divorce.

One of my beliefs is that our virtues are our values in action. Before you can live your values, you must identify and define them. Once you do, they can become a guide for almost every aspect of your life.

When you are aware of and live according to your values, you can curate your life so that where you work and live, and who you spend time with align with what matters to you.

When I set out to convert my ex's workspace into my office, I consider what is important to me. Esthetics matter! But the esthetics must align with the feeling I want to have when I enter my office. Stories and relationships are important to me. I can love a paint color, but I won't use it if it has a name that is a turn-off to me.

Colors like Dead Salmon or Mole's Breath are eliminated immediately. Why? Because they conjure up images and feelings that don't align with what's important to me. Chartreuse, on the other hand, means fun, liveliness, and vitality. Guess what color my mom and I choose for the back of the house and the color I paint two walls in my office?

In my Destination Clutter Cleanse™ program, I ask the question: Have you ever walked into someone's home and thought, *This doesn't look like them*? Or *this feels exactly like I expected their home to feel*? Either way, that is your subconscious assessing alignment between how that person shows up and how they appear to live—from your perspective. It is possible to appreciate the beauty of a space and still feel that it isn't right for you.

What about you? Do the rooms in your home feel like you? Are you living in alignment with what is important to you? What about your friends? The work you do and the space where you work? Are you showing up in the world aligned with your values?

As painful as the end of my relationship is, I know it is the healthiest thing for me because it doesn't reflect what's important to me in a relationship. Communication, appreciation, and emotional connection are important to me. Any relationship that doesn't honor that is out of alignment, and I must decide if I want to invite misalignment into my life or allow it to stay when I identify it.

Communication

My mother once told me that communication, or lack thereof, is a key factor in almost every relationship that ends poorly. This is true between partners, parents and children, siblings, and friends. Good communication is essential to establishing, maintaining, and enhancing healthy relationships.

Communicating confidently will be less daunting when you are comfortable being accountable and living in alignment with what matters to you. Virtue is when you live according to your values.

Knowledge alone does not result in living in alignment. Many people know the benefits of healthy eating yet continue to eat poorly. When a person embodies a value, it manifests as virtue. Embodiment is "the representation or expression of something tangibly or visibly." To embody nutritional living is to demonstrate one's nutritional knowledge through behavior.

When that internal shift happens, you will feel a certain way about yourself and how you show up. That feeling is what I call the flow of living in your life's stream. Once there, you will find it difficult to hold on to feelings of guilt or shame because you will be secure in who you are and how you're showing up in the world and for the world. That confidence creates a foundation for effective communication.

This is not a head game; it's a heart thing. Ask yourself: How will it feel to show up in the world leading your best self forward? This question applies even when things aren't going well, and there will be days when that's the case. Acknowledge and honor your feelings on those days.

The objective is for you to communicate from a real place. And be honest about your emotions. Have you ever told someone you were "fine" when you weren't? If you did, you likely followed up by pretending to be fine, so your behavior aligned with the lie. This is a how we embody a lie.

This is why the first step is being honest with yourself. Do this, and you can build a foundation that supports you in communicating more clearly, comfortably, and confidently.

Trust

By now, you see the connection between Accountability, Alignment, and Communication. When these things are in practice—not perfection, but practice—you will be positioned to trust.

Years ago, when I considered becoming a coach, I thought about how I would use learning and development from my higher education and corporate work experiences to support individuals in their personal and relationship development.

Working with Rodney Patterson, CEO of The Learner's Group, a friend, one of my support team members, and a business associate, I was introduced to Steven M.R. Covey's Speed of Trust®. Covey teaches that trust is an accelerator. The more trust between individuals, the more productive they can be in the workplace. This is as true in our personal and romantic relationships as it is in corporate environments.

Unlike respect, which should be given because of who you are and how you want to show up, trust must be earned. And because trust can be earned, it can also be violated and lost. One of the most damaging aspects of being in a failed relationship, particularly if it was toxic, is how it often destroys our ability to trust Self. Trust is the anchor leg of my A.A.C.T. In Joy! framework because of how personal, powerful, and pivotal it is in our lives.

There was a time when I saw myself as a failure whenever a relationship failed. I saw "picking wrong" as an indication that my judgement was defective. And if that were true, and we all get what we deserve, then I must not be worthy of a healthy, loving relationship. I realize how my distrust of Self became a source of self-doubt, indecisiveness, lack of confidence, insecurity, and more.

Here are a few things to consider and questions you can ask yourself to assess your ability to trust YOU:

Seeking External Validation: Can you make decisions without consulting several people around you?

Fear of Failure: Do you avoid making decisions for fear of being wrong?

Overthinking: Do you second-guess your decisions and actions and overthink them afterward?

Perfectionism: Are you afraid to start something if you don't see it ending perfectly?

Procrastination: Do you put things off waiting for that perfect time or until you can convince yourself that it will turn out perfectly? I call procrastination, perfectionisms cousin.

Negative Self-Talk: Are you guilty of thinking that erodes your self-confidence?

Unable to Make Decisions: Is decision making, even making minor decisions, a struggle for you?

Impulsive Behavior: Do you make quick decisions without considering the outcome because you don't trust your judgement?

Overriding Your Opinion/Overreliance on Others: Do you defer to other people's opinions even though you have strong feelings about what is best for you?

Weak or Non-Existent Boundaries: Do you struggle to assert yourself personally or professionally because you're afraid of conflict or being rejected?

Ignoring Your Intuition/Gut/Discernment: Do you dismiss your internal signal that something is wrong or needs attention?

Avoid Responsibility: Do you shy away from taking responsibility for your actions or decisions and the consequences, especially when it's an easy option?

Lack of Self-Compassion: When you make a mistake or face challenges, are you overly critical of yourself?

Hesitate Pursuing Objectives: Are your aspirations and dreams waiting on you because you feel paralyzed or hesitant?

Difficulty Expressing Your Needs: Do you experience anxiety that prevents you from communicating your needs in personal or professional situations?

Constant Self-Comparison: Do you measure your worth based on external benchmarks and compare yourself to others?

Constant Anxiety: Do you feel unsure about your ability to handle whatever comes your way?

Whew! Yes, that is a long list. If you have been telling yourself that you cannot trust people, people constantly let you down, or you can only depend on yourself, you likely have difficulty trusting others. And that could be tied to the last item on the list—**Constant Anxiety.**

Wait! Before you say anything or finish that thought of resistance that popped into your head, hear me out.

If your first thought was, *No, I can deal with things just fine. I don't trust other people to do the right thing!* —then this is for you. And thank you for letting me use you as an example.

I'm going to challenge you to consider something. Trusting yourself means that no matter what someone does or doesn't do, you know you will be fine because you can handle the outcome. If, however, you consistently position yourself to control the process and the outcome, that's not demonstrating trust—that's an attempt at exercising control.

In my *Divorce Is Not A Destination* program, I walk clients through A.A.C.T. We examine how items on the previous list can be connected. Constant Anxiety can lead to Ignoring Intuition, and Ignoring Intuition can lead to an Overreliance on Others. An Overreliance on Others can foster Difficulty Setting Boundaries.

For me, learning to trust that I could handle whatever came my way had everything to do with trusting that God is in control. And since he gave me dominion over things, I need to muster up the courage to be a good steward. For me, that begins with trusting and believing this:

I'm the right woman for the job of living my life.

Empowering Reflection

I have the right to take accountability for my life by living in alignment, being confident and clear when I communicate, and trusting myself to make value-based decisions on my behalf.

CHAPTER 11

Divorced and Dynamic

"Above all be the heroine of your life, not the victim."

— NORA EPHRON

Divorce is often viewed as a period of upheaval and uncertainty in life, and it's true that going through a divorce can be challenging. However, experiences change over time, and there's real potential for life to improve significantly if you believe it can.

Having studied women's experiences and mentoring extensively, I understand the importance of having role models who inspire and guide us through tough times. If you're struggling to find such a figure in your life, consider this chapter a gift. Each woman featured here has achieved remarkable success in her field while dealing with divorce, often in the public eye.

Fame and wealth don't shield anyone from heartache, disappointment, or loss. There's no quick fix for rebuilding confidence or finding joy after the end of a difficult relationship. Yet, each woman listed here has her own unique divorce story – a story of both struggle and triumph, much like you and me.

To be dynamic means embracing positivity, innovation, and energy despite life's challenges. As you read these remarkable stories, let them empower you to take the next step on your journey. I hope you grow to stand on your own story, transforming it into a beacon of encouragement and hope for others.

May you be encouraged by these extraordinary women.

Adelle: In Harmony With Self

Adelle's divorce marked a pivotal turning point in her life, both personally and professionally. She took her divorce experience and created what has become known as "the divorce album." She has shared that the music was also a message to her son, needed to help her communicate with him as he struggled with his parent's divorce.

Despite the emotional turmoil and challenges she faced during this period, Adelle emerged from the experience with a newfound sense of resilience and determination. Channeling her emotions into her music, she poured her heart and soul into her songs, creating raw and soul-stirring melodies that resonated with millions around the world. Through her honesty and vulnerability, Adelle connected with her audience on a profound level and garnered widespread acclaim and success in the music industry.

Her ability to transform personal pain into artistic brilliance became the cornerstone of her meteoric rise to fame, solidifying her status as one of the most influential and iconic artists of her generation. Adelle's journey serves as a powerful reminder of the transformative power of resilience and the enduring strength that lies within each of us, even in the face of adversity.

Yolanda Adams: Empowering Hearts and Minds Through Music

Her talent is such, that she has at least three titles, Queen of Contemporary Gospel, the First Lady of Modern Gospel, and the Reigning Queen of Urban Gospel. Ms. Yolanda Adams' journey includes two divorces. Her gifts and talents have garnered a myriad of awards that include four Grammy's and sixteen Stellar Gospel Music Awards. She is a mother, actor, inspirational speaker, and a testament to the transformative power of faith, resilience, and the healing power of music.

Lucille Ball: Television Comedy's Queen

Lucille Ball's indomitable spirit and comedic genius not only revolutionized the television industry but also inspired generations of women to embrace their unique talents and pursue their dreams fearlessly. She was the first woman filmed on television while visibly pregnant in real life.

Along with her first husband, she pioneered filming with a live audience using two cameras. Ms. Ball was the first woman to head a tv production company when she bought her ex's share of Desilu productions after their divorce in 1960. Ms. Ball remained married to her second husband until her death in 1989.

Drew Barrymore: Bloom's Wherever She's Planted

Drew Barrymore's evolution from child star to accomplished actress, producer, and entrepreneur is an inspiring testament to her unwavering determination to forge her own path to success. You could say she's blooming amazing with her lines of Flower Haircare tools, Flower Home and Flower Home Kids décor, Flower Eyewear, Flower Beauty products and a lifestyle book, Rebel Homemaker.

And because she doesn't live into her limitations, you can catch her bringing optimism, information, inspiration, and entertainment to daytime tv on, what else, *The Drew Barrymore Show*.

Halle Berry: Representation Matters and She Represents

She's been a Bond girl, won an Emmy, a Golden Globe, and played Dorothy Dandridge, the first Black actress nominated for an Academy Award for Best Actress. She then went on to become the first Black actress to win an Academy Award for Best Actress.

She's the proud mother of two children, a producer, philanthropist, and among the dozen or so charitable organizations she's been associated with, she is the first celebrity spokesperson for the Diabetes Awareness campaign. Halle Berry's journey through three marriages and divorces has not been easy, yet she has done it with grace, vulnerability, humor, and an unmatched zest for life.

Mary J. Blige: The Queen of Hip Hop Soul

Mary J. Blige, known as the Queen of Hip Hop Soul, has defied odds and risen to acclaim despite early challenges. She made history as the first person to be nominated for an Academy Award for both acting and songwriting in the same year, achievements that seemed distant during her childhood marked by sexual abuse and leaving high school.

However, her personal life saw struggles, notably her marriage of nearly a dozen years ending in divorce. Despite a prenuptial agreement, financial stress mounted with orders to pay her ex's legal fees, retroactive spousal support exceeding $200,000, and $30,000 monthly in alimony. The song *Rent Money* poignantly reflects her struggles to make ends meet during this time.

Ironically, Mary J.'s album also featured *Good Morning Gorgeous,* a reminder of self-love amid self-doubt. Her transparency and immense talent resonate with fans globally. She's received nine Grammys, an Emmy, four American Music Awards, twelve NAACP Image Awards, and twelve Billboard Music Awards. A successful transition to acting, earned her Golden Globe and Academy Award nominations. Through her journey, Mary J. Blige continues to inspire with her resilience and unwavering passion for music and artistry.

Kelly Brianne (Clarkson): Overcoming Heartache to Inspire Millions

From *American Idol* to international sensation. Kelly Brianne changed her name because of an estranged relationship with her father. The divorce from her ex, led to a $2.6 million dollar ruling in her favor for funds allegedly procured through illegal business dealings while her ex was acting in the capacity of her manager.

The pain from one relationship and hope for the love she desired in the other, can be felt in her single, "Piece by Piece." Resilience is her superpower. In addition to being the mother of two young children, she launched a successful talk show career. As host of *The Kelly Clarkson Show* she has received seven Daytime Emmy Awards including, Outstanding Entertainment Talk Show Host and Outstanding Talk Show Entertainment.

Ella Fitzgerald: The Jazz Legend Saved by Her Voice

Included amongst the many personal challenges she faced, was being orphaned after her mother's death. Young Ella was institutionalized after being charged with "incorrigibility." She would spend time in the Colored Orphanage in the Bronx, NY and eventually get transferred to a reformatory in Hudson, NY.

They say your gift will make a way for you. That's what happened to Ella when she was discovered after entering a talent contest at the famed Apollo Theater in Harlem, NY. You can say the rest is history. Ms. Fitzgerald soared to unprecedented heights in her career, captivating audiences worldwide with her unparalleled talent and grace. She was married twice and there is speculation of a third marriage. Among the numerous awards, Ella Fitzgerald won 13 Grammys and the Grammy's Lifetime Achievement Award.

Jasmine Guy: A Class Act

Jasmine Guy is an acclaimed actress, singer, director, and dancer. Her iconic role as Whitley Gilbert-Wayne earned her four NAACP Image Awards for Outstanding Lead Actress in a Comedy Series. Ms. Guy has admitted to having gone through a difficult and painful divorce that led to her filing for bankruptcy. Good fortune and her undeniable talent brought her work on shows like *Vampire Diaries, Grey's Anatomy, Harlem,* and two films on my holiday watch list, *A Wesley Christmas*, and a *Wesley Christmas Wedding.* Ms. Guy continues to delight old fans and garner new ones touring HBCU's with former cast members of *A Different World.*

Jennifer Hudson: When You EGOT It, You Got It

Jennifer Hudson, rose to fame as a finalist on *American Idol* before achieving critical acclaim for her role in "Dreamgirls." Jennifer persevered after facing the tragic loss of her mother, brother, and nephew. She is divorced from her ex, and together they have one child.

In 2022, she joined an exclusive group of fewer than two dozen industry icons when she earned an EGOT (Emmy, Grammy, Oscar, and Tony) for producing the Tony Award winning musical, A Strange Loop. Her talk show, *The Jennifer Hudson Show,* rose to the second most watched talk show among women between 18 and 34, and was recently renewed for its third season.

Janet Jackson: Rhythm, Resilience, and Music Royalty

Janet Jackson, an iconic singer, actress, and performer, who has sold more than 100 million records worldwide and is the recipient of dozens of awards including the American Music Award's "Award of Merit," Billboard Award's "Artistic Achievement Award," MTV's "Video Vanguard Award," and Recording Academy's "Governor's Award." Add to that list, MTV's inaugural Icon tribute, and Radio Music Award's "Legend and World Music Awards' "Legend Award". Jackson is ranked as the most-searched person in internet history. Her humanitarian efforts have garnered APLA's "Commitment to Life Award," amfAR's "Award of Courage," and GLAAD's "Vanguard Award."

Ms. Jackson has been married and divorced three times. During her third marriage, at the age of 50, she gave birth to her son. Janet continues to thrive in her career, inspiring generations with her music and performances.

Sheila Johnson: Trailblazers Do What Trailblazers Do

In the annals of history, the narratives of remarkable women often intersect with those of influential men. Sheila Johnson and her former husband co-founded BET. No matter how the spotlight found her, it is her resilience, determination, and unwavering commitment to excellence that propelled her onto a path of empowerment and impact.

Today, Ms. Johnson is the owner of The Salamander Resort & Spa in Virginia. The Salamander opened in 2013 and is now one of seven hotel properties in her portfolio. In addition to being a trailblazing entrepreneur, she supports the arts, education, youth, health, and human services & global development through The Sheila C. Johnson Foundation.

Gayle King: The Voice of Compassion and Good Sense Parenting

Gayle King is a highly respected journalist and television personality known for her role as a co-anchor on *CBS Mornings*, formerly *CBS This Morning*. Beyond her well-known friendship with Oprah Winfrey, Gayle King has established herself as a successful journalist and editor-at-large for O, The Oprah Magazine. She is celebrated for her insightful interviews with top newsmakers and celebrities.

In her personal life, Ms. King has been candid about her experiences as a single mother and co-parenting her children following the end of her eleven-year marriage. While she has shared that her marriage ended because her ex-husband was not monogamous, she demonstrates grace and respect for his privacy, by not divulging his name publicly.

In 2019, Ms. King's contributions to journalism were recognized with her induction into the Broadcasting and Cable Hall of Fame, highlighting her significant impact on the media industry. She continues to inspire and inform audiences with her professionalism, integrity, and engaging storytelling on television and in print.

Regina King: Reigning and Regal in Hollywood and In Life

Regina King has grown from the child actor in the hit tv sitcom, *227* to an Emmy and Academy Award-winning actress and director. She garnered widespread acclaim for her performances in films like *Ray* and television series like the *Watchmen*. Her role in *If Beale Street Could Talk*, led to her winning an Academy Award for Best Supporting Actress. Regina made a name for herself in her directorial debut with the critically acclaimed film, *One Night in Miami*.

Regina made the conscious decision to remove the wedge lodged between her and her ex after a messy breakup and divorce. It wasn't easy, but for the benefit of their son, she extended an olive branch to her ex, so they could be the co-parents he needed. She didn't want their son to experience the same emotional discord she had after her parent's divorced. Sadly, in 2022, Ms. King lost her son Ian to suicide.

Ms. King remains a powerhouse in the entertainment industry, breaking barriers and inspiring others with her talent, grace, and determination.

Eartha Kitt: The Most Exciting Woman in The World

Described by Orson Welles as "the most exciting woman in the world," Eartha Kit led a remarkable life filled with talent, perseverance, and activism.

Born to a mother of African-American and Cherokee descent, Ms. Kitt never knew the identity of her white father. It's believed she was conceived when her mother was raped. The lifelong uncertainty about her father's identity left a deep scar on Eartha Kitt.

One of Ms. Kitt's memorable roles was as Catwoman in the third season of the *Batman* television series (1967-1968), making her the first black woman to portray this iconic character on screen. Her portrayal brought a unique and captivating energy to the role.

In 1968, Eartha Kitt attended a luncheon at the White House hosted by Lady Bird Johnson, where she voiced criticism against the Vietnam War. Her outspokenness during this event had repercussions on her career in the United States, leading to a decline in opportunities. Facing adversity in the U.S., Ms. Kitt moved to Europe where she experienced a resurgence in her career and became an international sensation. Fluent in multiple languages, she captivated audiences with her singing and acting talents.

Eartha Kitt was briefly married to Bill McDonald, whom she divorced citing mental cruelty. They had one daughter named Kitt Shapiro.

Today, Kitt Shapiro honors her mother's legacy through "Simply Eartha," a lifestyle brand celebrating Eartha Kitt's artistry and impact.

Eartha Kitt's life is a testament to her strength, creativity, and ability to overcome obstacles. She remains an iconic figure remembered not only for her talents but also for her courage in speaking out against injustice.

Gladys Knight: The Empress of Soul

Gladys Knight began her musical journey at an early age, forming the group Gladys Knight and the Pips with two siblings and two cousins. The group quickly gained recognition for their captivating performances and soulful harmonies, achieving great success with hits like *Midnight Train to Georgia* and *Neither One of Us (Wants to Be the First to Say Goodbye)*. The group was inducted into the Rock and Roll Hall of Fame in 1996.

Despite personal challenges, including four marriages, three of which ended in divorce, Gladys Knight remains committed to her music, continues to perform, and has added producer and actress to her credits with roles in numerous television shows and films like *Coming to America 2*.

Gladys's enduring legacy as a music icon is marked by her 13 Grammy Awards and her ability to touch the hearts of audiences worldwide with her soul-stirring voice and emotive performances. Her contributions to soul music and her resilience in overcoming obstacles continue to inspire generations of artists and music lovers alike.

Hoda Kotb: Finding Joy and Purpose Amidst Life's Challenges

Hoda Kotb's journey has inspired millions. Following her divorce and subsequent challenges, including her battle with breast cancer, Ms. Kotb found solace and strength in her role as a mother. Together, she and her ex-fiancé are parents to two adopted daughters.

As a co-anchor NBC's *Today Show*, Ms. Kotb's conversational interview style and compassionate disposition have earned her numerous accolades, including a Daytime Emmy Award and a Webby Award for her interview featuring Viola Davis on her *Making Space with Hoda Kotb* podcast.

In addition to her impactful television career, Hoda Kotb is also a prolific author. One of her notable books is titled *I Really Needed This Today: Words to Live By*, which features inspirational quotes and stories aimed at providing encouragement and positivity to readers. She has also authored children's books, including *I've Loved You Since Forever* and *You Are My Happy*, which celebrate themes of love, joy, and family.

Jennifer Lopez (J Lo): When You Realize It's Your Story to Tell

You may know her as J Lo, Jenny from the Block, or that dancer on from In Living Color. The singer, dancer, actress, producer, and choreographer recently debuted *This is Me... Now: A Love Story*, a cinematic, musical reimagining of her love life. That includes four marriages and three divorces. Today, the mother of two is reunited and married to a former boyfriend. Fans and non-fans alike may be drawn in by the vulnerability Lopez demonstrates in taking on a project of such magnitude in a way that pokes fun at her own journey of love, loves lost, and love found.

Diana Ross: Motown Royalty Who Reached Out and Touched The World

Diana Ross, often referred to as the "Queen of Motown," is a legendary singer, actress, and record producer. Named "Female Entertainer of the Century" by Billboard in 1976, she is the only woman artist to have had number-one pop singles on Billboard's Hot 100 in the U.S. as a solo artist, and as part of a duet, a trio, and an ensemble. Add to that two Grammy Lifetime Achievement Awards as a solo artist and a member of the Supremes.

Her unparalleled success came behind hits like *Ain't No Mountain High Enough, I'm Coming Out,* and her signature song, *Reach Out and Touch (Somebody's Hand).* Diana has been married twice. She has one child with Motown Founder, and two children with each of her two husbands. Both marriages ended in divorce.

Ms. Ross recently celebrated her 80th birthday and she continues to wow audiences with her performances.

Jill Scott: Soulful Sounds, Heart Inspired Living

A Philadelphia native, Jill Scott was raised by her mother and grandmother. She left college when she realized that becoming a teacher was no longer the path for her. She's gone on to become a Grammy Award-winning singer-songwriter, actress, and poet, who has captivated audiences with her soulful voice and empowering lyrics.

Ms. Scott has one child with an ex-fiancé. She has been married and divorced twice and has said that she views her first husband as a husband. Her second spouse of nearly 18-months, she refers to it as nonconsequential. True to her nature, she continues to believe in love, saying that she's learned to give people the time to reveal themselves.

Beyond her music career, Jill has excelled as an actress, with roles in films like Tyler Perry's *Why Did I Get Married?* and television series like *The No. 1 Ladies' Detective Agency.* She also created the Blue Babe Foundation, a Philadelphia based organization that offers scholarship and mentoring for students. Part of Blue Babe Foundation is Camp Jill Scott, a free one-day camp that provides fun outdoor experiences for young scholars in North Philadelphia.

Martha Stewart: From Caterer to Creative Mogul

Many don't know that Martha Stewart was married for nearly 30-years. She and her ex have one daughter. A CNN documentary on Martha revealed that after their divorce in 1990, her ex married her assistant who was 21-years his junior. Ms. Stewart has been quoted as saying her divorce was terrible. Partly because she was the first person in her family to get divorced.

More than a decade later, Martha was convicted for lying and obstructing justice regarding the sales of ImClone Systems stock. She served five months in prison, followed by five months of home detention.

Ms. Stewart founded Omnimedia, an umbrella organization for various media and merchandising ventures connected to the Martha Stewart brand. She continued to serve as chief creative officer of Omnimedia after it was acquired by Sequential Brands for approximately $350 million.

Tina Turner: When You Truly Believe It – Nothing Else Matters

Tina Turner's journey to becoming the Queen of Rock 'n' Roll is nothing short of miraculous. After surviving years in an abusive marriage, she set herself free, inspiring countless others to believe that freedom was possible for them as well. She accomplished all this while also being a single mother.

At the age of 44, she took the music industry and fans around the world by storm with a feat few thought possible. Her comeback album "Private Dancer," solidified her as an international superstar.

From *Proud Mary* to *What's Love Got to Do with It*, Tina's anthem-like messages resonated with the masses and made her a global phenomenon for decades. Her album "Private Dancer" earned multi-platinum certifications in countries around the world and was selected by the Library of Congress for preservation in the National Recording Registry due to its cultural, historical, and aesthetic significance.

In addition to her musical achievements, Tina's journey towards self-discovery and inner peace led her to embrace Buddhism, which became an integral part of her life and spirituality. Her practice of Buddhism provided her with strength, resilience, and a sense of purpose, guiding her through both triumphs and challenges.

Iyanla Vanzant: Helping Hearts Heal, Including Her Own

Before becoming a renowned inspirational speaker, spiritual teacher, and author, Iyanla Vanzant graduated with the inaugural class of the City University Law School at Queens College. She worked for three years as an attorney for the Public Defender's office in Philadelphia, until the day she walked away from her desk and never returned.

Ms. Vanzant embarked on a journey of self-discovery and spiritual awakening, eventually finding her calling in helping others navigate their own paths to healing. Her ability to help others did not shield her from personal hardships. She has been unemployed and lost a million-dollar home to foreclosure while going through a divorce. After nine years, she discontinued a her successful tv show, *Iyanla Fix My Life*. She decided that her freedom was more important to her, and she opted to remove the negative energy that came through cyberbullying that included death threats.

Ms. Vanzant has lived a parent's nightmare by having to bury her two daughters. Today, she is married and has one adult child from a previous marriage. She has authored seventeen books and is a six-time New York Times bestselling author. She's the recipient of four

NAACP Image Awards and has three honorary degrees. Fortunately, she continues to coach and inspire millions around the world.

Reese Witherspoon: Reading is Fundamental

Reese Witherspoon has three children from two marriages. Ms. Witherspoon has not been defined or debilitated by her divorces. In 2021 Forbe's reported that Reese was one of the world's highest paying actresses. In 2023 she was named one of the richest women in America.

She is an actress, producer, and advocate for women's rights who has actively and intentionally created a path for other women to find their way to success. Reese's Book Club is run under her media company Hello Sunshine. Several books selected for the book club have been adapted to film, giving the work of female authors a visibility they otherwise would not have received and the world an opportunity to experience the perspectives and experiences of women we otherwise wouldn't have known.

Dynamically YOU!

Through their resilience, determination, and unwavering spirit, these remarkable women have not only overcome the challenges of divorce but have emerged as dynamic forces in their respective fields. Their stories serve as sources of inspiration and empowerment, reminding us that adversity is not a barrier to success but rather a steppingstone to greatness. Use their achievements as reminders of what's possible.

Now, it's time for you to add your name to the list. Be the heroine in your life by learning to tell your own story. Put your name on the line below and write a short story about yourself, similar to the ones you just read. Count on you. Bet on you. Believe in you. You are worthy.

Write Your Name Here

_____

_____

_____

_____

_____

_____

_____

_____

_____

_____

_____

_____

_____

_____

CHAPTER 12

Journey to Joy

"My mission in life is not merely to survive, but to thrive; and to do so with some passion, some compassion, some humor, and some style."

— MAYA ANGELOU

"He only wants to marry you to get a green card."

"Getting married in Africa!? What will you do next, put a ring in your nose?"

"If it was me . . ."

These comments are made during a time when I expected people to be happy for my happiness. One time, it was during a phone call. The others during those infrequent visits when you gather with friends and family you don't see or speak with regularly. Usually, sharing wedding plans is met with excitement and congratulations. Not necessarily the case when it's your third wedding and you're marrying an African you met the previous year on a mission trip.

The comments sting. I don't retaliate verbally, at first. Perhaps I'm shocked, then sorely disappointed because I expect better from people close to me. The first comment I attribute to jealousy and self-loathing. It isn't shared out of concern. But why would I expect someone who doesn't seem very happy with their life to find joy in me living mine?

The *nose ring* comment, although enveloped in sarcastically dry humor, is not funny. As they say, timing is everything. That comment, I attribute to fear and ignorance. Fear of a place they've never been. Ignorance, because even in jest, it was heavy with the socialization that depicts Africans and their traditions as barbaric and native in the most negative and undignified of ways.

The third comment? Let's just say *I had time* that day.

"If it was me ..." had all the markings of the beginning of a *let me get on my soapbox and tell you what you ought to be doing* lecture.

I didn't let them finish the sentence.

"It *isn't* you. It's me. My life, my choice. God didn't present you with this opportunity so there's no point in you talking about 'If it was me ...'"

A few seconds of discomfort filled the silence before another family member cleared the air by changing the subject. But that is the last negative comment I ever hear about my pending nuptials.

The future ex of this marriage is intelligent, easy spoken, mature beyond his years, and strikingly handsome. He speaks three languages, once taught math at a nearby school, and is an interpreter for our group. One of my favorite pictures of him is his profile as he stands on a bridge in Burundi, looking off into the distance.

Although taken by surprise, my parents are supportive and agree to return with me to Rwanda for the wedding. My oldest friend in the world, Olivia, agrees to be my maid of honor and fulfills a lifelong dream of hers to visit Africa.

The marriage is fraught with challenges. Some, the garden variety. Others include being separated for 18 months as his family dealt with issues that left him unable to get a passport. Mounting frustration, family dynamics, the distance, and financial issues all but guaranteed that by the time he arrives in the U.S., our first months together as a married couple would be our last.

While in Rwanda for the wedding, my mother befriends an American living there with his wife, a Burundian native. Together, they are rehabilitating a defunct fish nursery to create jobs for community members and provide food for the region.

Her friendship gets us invited to the property for lunch. It is a magnificent place. Sitting on the property, surrounded by lush green foliage has me thinking, *This must be what that Garden of Eden looked like.*

My dad and Jon hit it off. The two of them talk about so much that Jon makes an offer my father can't refuse. My mother excuses herself to go inside to the restroom. My dad seizes the opportunity.

Perry leans across the table and says, "Hey, Leese, I need you to talk to your mom about something."

"Ok, what is it?" Leaning in to hear his whisper.

"I need you to convince her to let me stay here and work on the nursery with Jon for three months."

"You just came back from missing Christmas after sailing down the Mexican coastline from California. If she goes for this, she's going to revoke your passport when you get back home."

The truth is I'm so excited about this opportunity for my dad that selling the idea to my mom doesn't take long. After all, we are literally sitting in a garden, in Rwanda, because I decided to marry a Rwandan interpreter who I met less than 12 months ago.

Yes, we ended up divorced. And it was not amicable. Still, I can honestly say, I'd do it all over again for my dad to have the experience he had in Rwanda. For the rest of his life, anytime he talked about the people, and their appreciation for him and his for them, his eyes glistened.

He'd say, "I never even imagined going to Africa. And to have spent that time there and to feel so welcomed, I can't tell you what that meant to me."

Before you run off and marry someone so a family member can have a once-in-a-lifetime experience, keep reading. If your divorce has happened, perhaps you need to stop looking at the divorce and look at what good came about because of the marriage. What good experiences did you have? What places did you visit because of the relationship? Did you meet people who left positive impressions on you? Have you created friendships that will outlive the relationship? Did you have children? All these things and much more should be looked at as blessings that came about because of the relationship.

As I write this chapter, I'm sitting on my sofa. Looking up, I see a carving depicting a celebratory scene of Rwandans dancing and playing instruments. Just beyond that, on a wall further away, hangs a mask. Its eyes are closed. The narrow face is relaxed and smiling. The warm brown wood is crowned with a traditional Rwandese hairstyle.

Both pieces make me smile. I feel good when I see them. One is from my first trip with the missionary group. The other is one my mother purchased when she and my dad came for my wedding. Neither of them leaves me sitting in sadness, ruminating over the marriage that ended.

These pieces represent the love and joy of my experiences, rather than the hurt and pain associated with a relationship that ran its course. Besides, after four marriages, if I got rid of everything in my home that reminded me of an ex, I'd be sitting on the floor right now.

Joy Comes in the Morning

There was a time when I would listen to speakers talk about how difficult and horrible their lives had been, and it made me question if I really had anything to overcome that would inspire others. Acutely aware of and grateful for my middle-class upbringing, I felt I needed a rags to riches, devastation to dynamic, horrible to hilltop experience to be credible. That was me not trusting myself and not honoring the voice inside of me that whispered, *somebody else needs to hear this.*

We all deal with situations that have the potential to derail us. We don't benefit from comparing our experiences to anyone else's. The fact is, I've lived through difficult decisions, like choosing abortion, and horrible situations I didn't choose, like being raped, sexually assaulted, robbed at gunpoint, and having my car stolen. And all those things have happened more than once.

I know what you're thinking: Who gets robbed at gunpoint more than once!? And one of the robberies was a bank robbery!

One of the most challenging things I've dealt with is being diagnosed with scoliosis. It is the summer before my freshman year of high school. I am devastated because everything is devastating at 14. It is also excruciatingly painful. Scoliosis is a sideways curvature of the spine. One of the curves in my "S" shaped spine happens to be curved at 32 degrees, which is 4 degrees away from requiring surgery. It has pinched a nerve so badly that I'm not able to move my legs the night I'm taken to the hospital. Treatment is physical therapy and wearing a Milwaukee Brace all four years of high school.

Like you, I've made mistakes, have regrets, and have not always been fair or treated fairly. I've loved, been loved, experienced heartache, and have been told of the heartache I've caused others. I've lived long enough to be ok with the fact that life doesn't promise us fair.

If you're wondering: *Is she going to go into detail about the rapes, the robberies, her abortions …?* The answer is *no*. The reason is because I couldn't figure out how the details would serve you. And in that, there's one more lesson: You can be vulnerable and honest without oversharing.

There will be people in my family and close circle of friends who won't know as much as you just learned about me unless they read this book. I wrote *Divorce Is Not A Destination* to give you tools and encouragement so you can more confidently address challenges and grow from adversity.

International Speaker Lisa Nichols would say that I'm able to share what I share because I'm at a place in my life where I can stand on my story and not be stuck in it. This is what I wish for you. It is a wonderful gift you can give to yourself.

Destined for Joy

Believe life is happening *to* you, and you open the door to feeling like a victim, held hostage by your own life. From this vantage point you will see difficulties as hardships outside of your control. Problems will confound and weaken you, dampening your ability to overcome them.

Live as though life is happening *for* you, and you live empowered, expecting to get through it, whatever *it* is. One experience doesn't define you even if that experience is a breakup or divorce. Only you define what your experiences represent in your life. Post-traumatic growth will not happen without difficulties.

Examine the past to learn from it; don't live in it.

Divorce is not a destination it is an experience. Make your destination joy, and you will always be on the right path.

I will leave you with a poem I wrote a few years ago. Let it remind you that life continues after divorce, and you have all you need to take the next step on your journey.

On and On and On

I awoke to this thing called life
not understanding how I fit into its landscape.
With its rising mountains and rough terrain, I walked through
meadows filled with sunshine and forests bathed by rain.

Redwoods growing into the heavens
amidst fires that crumbled some to their knees.
Marveled that time went on and on and on.

I learned to embrace life when I learned to love on me.
I awoke to the mysteries of not knowing how a flower unfolds in
sunlight or how honey is made by bees.

I took delight in believing that Gods mysteries also live in me.
Who knows how I love the way I do.
How my heart's light always shines through.

Ahhh the wonders of life live in you too
 and yes, they go on and on and on.

© 2020 Lisa Summerour

Bibliography

Cuddy, Amy. 2018. *Presence: Bringing Your Boldest Self to Your Biggest Challenges*. New York: Back Bay Books.

Davis, Viola. 2022. *Finding Me*. HarperCollins.

Dweck, Carol S. 2016. *Carol Dweck's Mindset: The New Psychology of Success*. Ant Hive Media.

Erwin Raphael McManus. 2023. *Mind Shift*. Convergent Books.

Fessler, Ann. 2007. *The Girls Who Went Away: The Hidden History of Women Who Surrendered Children for Adoption in the Decades Before Roe V. Wade*. N.p.: Penguin Publishing Group.

Helmstetter, Shad. 2017. *What to Say When You Talk to Your Self*. New York: Gallery Books.

Katie, Byron, and Stephen Mitchell. 2021. *Loving What Is: Four Questions That Can Change Your Life*. New York: Potter/Ten Speed/Harmony/Rodale.

Kübler-Ross, Elisabeth. 1969. *On Death and Dying: What the Dying Have to Teach Doctors, Nurses, Clergy, and Their Own Families*. New York: Macmillan.

Kübler-Ross, Elisabeth, and David Kessler. 2014. *On Grief & Grieving: Finding the Meaning of Grief through the Five Stages of Loss*. London: Simon & Schuster.

Levine, Amir, and Rachel Heller. 2012. *Attached: The New Science of Adult Attachment and How It Can Help You Find - and Keep - Love*. Tarcherperigee.

Lifford, Tina. 2019. *The Little Book of Big Lies: A Journey Into Inner Fitness*. N.p.: Harper Collins.

Palmer, Anne. 2013. *The Gifted Trap E. M. E. R. G. E. From Gifted to Great*.

Phillips, Anita. 2023. *The Garden Within*. Thomas Nelson.

Raiford, Dalton Palmer. 2021. *I Just Want This Done: How Smart, Successful People Get Divorced without Losing Their Kids, Money, and Minds.* Elmhurst, Illinois: E. James Publishing Company, Inc.

Reeder, Caryn A. 2022. *The Samaritan Woman's Story.* InterVarsity Press.

Robbins, Mel. 2024. *The #1 Neuroscientist: After Listening to This, Your Brain Will Not Be the Same.* n.d. Accessed April 14, 2024. https://youtu.be/Uzt-Woc3CVk?feature=shared.

Spoerre, Anna. 2021. *Unwed Black Mothers in 20th Century Kansas City Found Refuge in Home for Women, Girls* | Kansas City Public Library. n.d. Kclibrary.org. Accessed April 6, 2024. https://kclibrary.org/news/2021-05/unwed-black-mothers-20th-century-kansas-city-found-refuge-home-women-girls.

Smith, Kristian A. 2022. *Breaking All the Rules.* Disruptive Enterprises.

Stark, Patricia. 2021. *Calmfidence.* Sounds True.

Strickland, Sheeka. 2015. *The Forgotten Home. Maternity homes have largely…* | by Sheeka Strickland. Medium. https://medium.com/@sheeka_s/the-forgotten-home-5b914565ddba.

Swart, Tara. 2019. *The Source : The Secrets of the Universe, the Science of the Brain.* New York, Ny: Harperone, An Imprint Of Harpercollins Publishers.

Turvey, Matthew, Psy Director, and David Olson. n.d. "A Marriage CoMission Research Report." https://rw360.org/wp-content/uploads/2017/04/Marriage-and-Family-Wellness-Corporate-America-1.pdf.

Wanberg, Connie R., Borbala Csillag, and Michelle K. Duffy. 2023. *After the break-up: How divorcing affects individuals at work.* Personnel Psychology 76 (1): 77

Connect

Summa Our Creatives, Inc.

www.DrLisaSummerour.com

www.DivorceIsNotADestination.com

Facebook: @drlisasummerour

Instagram: @drlisasummerour

YouTube: @drlisasummerour

Offerings & Resources

I honestly believe that no one will ever invest with you at a level higher than you are willing to invest in yourself. As a personal and professional coach, I always want to leave you with more than you expect. If you are an entrepreneur or someone wanting to transition to running your own business, below are a few of my offerings, and a list of resources that have been invaluable to me.

The Get Ready To Work Workbook™
www.grtwworkbook.com

Be More Confident, Calm, and Prepared For Your Next Job Interview. Often a breakup can initiate change in other areas of your life. Whether you're embarking on an entrepreneurial journey or changing careers, you may need to improve your interview skills. Be ready so you don't have to get read, with the Get Ready to Work Workbook. This second edition includes new sections on cover letters and steps you can take when you receive a job offer and when you do not. When you accept the job offer, there is an added section that guides you through maximizing the onboarding process.

Rebuilding Better Boundaries Challenge™
www.rebuildingbetterboundarieschallenge.com

Experience Emotional Freedom by Building Better Boundaries – Especially After a Breakup. If you've finished reading *Divorce Is Not A Destination*, you are ready for the Rebuilding Better Boundaries Challenge. Click the link to learn more and register for five-hours that will show you why you've been feeling guilty about taking care of yourself and give you the tools to stop!

Mia Redrick – The Chief Giant®
www.miaredrick.com

THE coach to help you package, position, price, and pitch your knowledge into a high-ticket service or sales offering. As a business owner, my experience with Mia was life-changing. As a woman, finding like-minded women willing to share thoughts, ideas, and knowledge was lifesaving! It was the professional life-line I didn't know I needed until I found it.

B.O.S.S. Moves by Myron Golden
https://affiliate.drlisasummerour.com/bossmoves

Business Optimization Success Secrets From a Million Dollar Round Table. B.O.S.S. Moves is a blueprint full of often missed and misunderstood business basics. Written by a man who has helped individuals have million-dollar weeks and days, it's for you if you are ready to position yourself for immeasurable success."

Make More Offers Challenge
https://affiliate.drlisasummerour.com/mmoc

This is a five-day experience that will literally challenge you to move your business forward. You will quickly realize the importance of making premium offers so the right clients can find you. This challenge will guide you in taking the pressure out of selling and replacing it with the immense pleasure you get from serving the people you were meant to serve.

Acknowledgements

A sincere thank you to Pastor Lisa Taylor for your friendship and the enlightening conversation that helped me align my life experiences with my education and purpose. Your insights have been invaluable.

Thank you to The Chief Giant®, Mia Redrick, for providing unprecedented mentoring and a supportive community that encouraged me to continue writing and challenged me to grow as an author. Your guidance has been instrumental in shaping my writing journey and my professional development.

A huge appreciation goes to book writing coach Teresa de Grosbois for the transformative weeklong experience. Your coaching will undoubtedly yield benefits for years to come, enhancing both my skills as a writer and my approach to storytelling.

To Bonita, thank you for sharing your story and inspiring me to view my own from a different perspective. Your courage has had a profound impact on my narrative and writing process.

Heartfelt gratitude to my parents, my unofficial first readers in life, for their unwavering support and inspiration. Your encouragement has fueled my passion for writing and storytelling.

To my accountability sister-friends, my first coach Kath Schnorr and Dr. Gail, navigating the challenges of the pandemic and beyond was made bearable because of our weekly check-ins. Your support and friendship have been a constant source of strength and encouragement.

A special thanks to my sister April, my trusted confidante and first editor extraordinaire. Your keen eye, honest opinions, and thoughtful considerations have been invaluable throughout this journey.

I am deeply grateful to Sara Davison of The International Divorce Coaching Centre of Excellence and The Dash Charity for the compassionate learning experience and wealth of exposure to experts from around the world devoted to helping people through their breakups and divorces.

I extend my thanks to each client I've had the pleasure of working with and to every colleague I've had the honor to serve alongside. Your collaborations and shared experiences have enriched my understanding and expertise in ways I could never have imagined.

Finally, I offer my thanks to God for the blessings, gifts, and talents with which I've been entrusted. My aim is to always be a good steward of these gifts. While I may fall short at times, I am committed to never straying from the shelter of your grace and mercy.

About the Author

 **Dr. Lisa Summerour** is the president of Summa Our Creatives, Incorporated and the creator of a suite of programs under the *Divorce Is Not A Destination* (DINAD) brand. Hosted on the Live Empowered Lead U platform, the DINAD programs are primarily tailored for women navigating personal and professional challenges before and after a breakup or divorce, including those recovering from difficult or toxic relationships.

Years ago, Dr. Lisa embarked on a journey that led her to become her own first client. Fortunately, her self-discovery didn't hinder her from enjoying success in various realms. An acting career allowed her to work alongside industry legends like Forrest Whitaker, Bruce Willis, and Denzel Washington. As a speaker, consultant, and facilitator, she's had the good fortune to travel to more than 30 states and 20 countries for business and pleasure. Crafting motivational speeches, she has presented to hundreds and thousands at U.S. sales conferences and designed curriculum for leaders from West Africa as a speaker for a leadership summit in Ghana.

While acquaintances may have admired Dr. Summerour's apparent lifestyle, few were aware of the challenges and traumas she endured along the way. She faced difficult breakups, emotional stress, and navigated the complexities of multiple marriages and divorces. Throughout these trials and more, Dr. Lisa diligently worked to overcome obstacles, often concealing the impact and related struggles.

It was the culmination of her life experiences, encouragement from those around her, and her passion to support others in living fully engaged lives that led her to develop what she wished she had access to during her relationship journeys: An organized, guided process that offers support, community, and confidentiality.

Through her programs, Dr. Summerour reassures and empowers others that they need not face similar challenges alone. Healing from heartache, rebuilding confidence, and living with joy after a breakup is within reach, and Dr. Summerour is committed to guiding others toward this transformation.

Dr. Lisa Summerour is a Master Practitioner breakup and divorce coach accredited by The International Divorce Coach Centre of Excellence and The Dash Charity, an organization supporting individuals experiencing domestic abuse for over 45 years. She is also a certified assessor of the Intercultural Conflict Style Inventory (ICS), a personal and professional coach, a certified IDI Administrator, and a certified Equitable Leader Assessment (ELA) administrator. Additionally, she is a member of the Screen Actors Guild/American Federation of Television & Radio Artists, the National Speakers Association, the North County African American Women's Association, and a certified member of the Pacific Southwest Minority Development Council. Dr. Summerour is the author of several books, a keynote speaker, enthusiastic traveler, seamstress, and avid DIYer.

Notes

Notes

Divorce Is Not A Destination®